CW01011510

Gaslighting

How to Deal with Gaslighting to Avoid Emotional Abuse and Psychological Manipulation

Declan Evans

Table of Contents

Introduction...4

Chapter 1: *Gaslighting*..5

Chapter 2: *How Can Gaslighting Affect You?*............................. 13

Chapter 3: *The Stages of Gaslighting* 17

Chapter 4: *Gaslighting in a Relationship*.................................. 23

Chapter 5: *Gaslighting Everywhere*... 26

Chapter 6: *Things Narcissists Say During Gaslighting* 36

Chapter 7: *Why Narcissists Prey on Intelligent People*............ 45

Chapter 8: *How to Handle the Effects of Gaslighting* 50

Chapter 9: *Powerful Ways to Disarm a Gaslighter*................... 55

Chapter 10: *Gaslighting Repellent: How to Shut Down a Narcissist* 62

Chapter 11: *Healing from Gaslighting* 68

Chapter 12: *Learn to be Strong*... 76

Chapter 13: *How a Gaslighter Will React When You Resist* 82

Chapter 14: *Self-Care* 89

Chapter 15: *Self-Love and Self-Care*... 95

Chapter 16: *Overcoming Gaslighting in Relationships*............. 97

Conclusion.. 109

Introduction

Gaslighting is emotional manipulation where the main aim of the abuser is to make you question your sanity. This gives the abuser the upper hand in the relationship, and they can make you do whatever they want to fulfill their ulterior motives. Contrary to what most people think, gaslighting is not only seen in personal or romantic relationships but is also very common in professional setups. With time, the victims start doubting themselves, and they become very sure that something is gravely wrong with them.

My aim in this book is to create a general awareness about gaslighting because that is the first thing you need to protect yourself from the gaslighters around you. The moment you learn to recognize it, you can arm yourself with strategies that will save you. When the gaslighter is someone very close to you or someone you trust, it becomes even more challenging to identify the signs of gaslighting, but I have explained how you can do so in this book.

Even if you have been a victim of gaslighting for years, healing is possible, and we will discuss that in this book. There are plenty of books on this subject on the market, so thanks for choosing this one! Every effort was made to ensure that it is full of helpful information. Please enjoy!

Chapter 1:
Gaslighting

A gaslighter wants to control another person and use them for their purposes. They do this by getting someone else to doubt their sanity and make them second guess themselves as a person.

Another way that gaslighting happens is when one partner tries to convince the other that their perception of reality is wrong or even telling the individual what's real versus what's not. For example, the gaslighting partner will say things like, "you're too sensitive" or "you imagine things. You're too unstable. You're deranged." They will also try to make the victim feel ashamed of themselves and their perceptions.

The origins of gaslighting are in an old play called Gas Light, made into a movie in the 1940s. The story is about a husband trying to drive his wife crazy, but she doesn't realize it until she finds out that her husband has been manipulating her perception of reality.

The term gaslighting comes from the old concept that you're driving someone insane by turning down the gaslights in their house. You're dimming the lights to make them think they're going crazy. That's what a gaslighter does in a relationship. They make you believe that you can't trust your mind or perceptions.

Gaslighting is very cruel, and it's difficult for a victim even to realize that it's happening because they don't understand how someone could be messing with their head like that.

Gaslighting is also a form of manipulative behavior used by abusers to control people. When someone is abusive, they make the victim believe they are unstable and then use that to manipulate them into doing what the abuser wants. For example, the abuser may make excuses for his or her behaviors while blaming the victim. An abuser might also make up lies and tell them to other people who believe the lies instead of considering the victim's story.

They will do this while at the same time telling them not to leave. They might also try and make the victim feel responsible for their abuse by saying, "you brought this on yourself." Finally, they might bring up the idea that they should leave because the gaslighting partner is good-looking and successful, but that the victim is unattractive and has no prospects.

Gaslighting is an intense form of abuse that does not allow room for a healthy relationship or healthy communication between two people.

Examples of Gaslighting

When a gaslighter is trying to get someone to question their sanity, they will make the victim believe they are crazy or overly emotional over little things. The gaslighter may accuse their partner of imagining things, being too sensitive, and even making up problems where there weren't any at all.

Gaslighters will commonly tell their partners exactly what they are doing while doing it to mess with their heads. For example, the gaslighter may say, "I'm not upset with you," right before showing they're upset about something the victim did. Another example is telling their partner not to be angry with them when they're angry.

When a gaslighter uses the silent treatment, they will do it for long periods. They will also use the silent treatment as a punishment for something their partner did, even if it was unintentional on their part. A gaslighter might also try and ignore a request from someone that has nothing to do with them.

A gaslighter may use other emotional tactics to manipulate their spouse. One of these tactics is guilt-tripping. They will tell their partner, "you're always saying hateful things about me" or something similar. They will do this in a way that makes the victim feel like they are at fault for their abuse, and it makes the victim second guess themselves as a person because if the gaslighter was being so horrible all of the time, why would anyone stay with them?

Gaslighters may try and make their partner wholly convinced that they have imagined something when they haven't said a word about it yet, or they may not say anything at all in an attempt to avoid conflict.

Standard Gaslighting Techniques You Need

Gaslighting happens to people worldwide and is a form of mental abuse that can make someone question their feelings, instincts, or sanity. It's a technique of twisting reality to serve one person's emotional needs at the expense of another. Gaslighting is often seen in relationships where one person has more power than another, such as with parents and children, or it can be seen between couples.

For gaslighting to be effective, the abuser needs to have some degree of trust from the victim. This allows the abuser to put doubt into their victim without the victim realizing it. The abuser may also use tactics like discounting, denial, or even blame to make their victim doubt themselves and look at things from their point of view. This type of abuse usually happens over a long period, possibly even years or decades.

Gaslighting can happen in any relationship that is based on power and control. It is used as a tool to gain access to resources like money, sex, food, and shelter.

- **Countering** - This is when someone denies they ever said something when they did. A prominent example of this would be when someone says, "I love you," and the other person replies, "I never said that." A less obvious example would be when someone buys something and asks for their money back, and the buyer says, "I never asked for my money back." No matter how blatant it is, the gaslighter will deny ever saying what they said.

- **Withholding** - This is when the abuser refuses to communicate with their victim. It can be very frustrating for victims because it gives the abuser control over them while still having access to their victim. It's also a type of punishment often used as leverage against them for some reason or another. This also occurs when their partner asks for the truth about something, and they reply with silence or will only reply with a question in return.

- **Denial/forgetting** - This is when the abuser claims that they don't remember what they did or who they talked to. Think of it as a time machine in that the abuser gets to relive something in their mind and deny it's happening. A good example is when someone asks their partner if they had talked to their ex, but they say they have no idea what their partner is talking about when asked.

- **Trivializing** - This is when the abuser tries to make a victim feel insignificant or even stupid. Again, it's used as a way to shame their victim or make them look bad in front of others.
- **Diversion/blocking** - This is when a person tries to get their victim to focus on something else. They might try to say that they're overreacting, too sensitive, or even crazy.
- **Stereotyping** is when the abuser assigns a negative trait to their victim, often one that isn't true. It can be anything from the person being lazy to a poor housekeeper to being annoying.

The purpose of gaslighting is to control and take away the victim's freedom by manipulating them into thinking they're crazy. Over time, gaslighting victims can become so confused about what is real and not that they start questioning their thoughts and feelings about certain situations. Instead, they might start believing things like they are not good enough or that everyone else hates them. This makes them feel isolated from their friends and family and ultimately leads to mental illness in some cases.

Signs of Gaslighting

- **Denial**

The first sign of gaslighting is that you get a sense that something isn't right, but when you try to talk about your feelings, the other person denies that anything is wrong. The other person will either deny that anything is wrong or tell you that you imagine things. They will turn the conversation around to make it all about how you are feeling.

They will say things like "I don't know what you're talking about" or "There's nothing wrong with me."

If one of these signs is present, then there is a reason to be suspicious. There may not be any gaslighting going on, but something is going on, and it should be discussed. It can help talk through your feelings with someone else who can listen objectively and give support and guidance.

- **White Lies**

The second sign of gaslighting is that you start to feel like you have to do a lot of explaining when you don't have to. So, for example, you can be talking about a movie, and the other person will say, "Oh yeah, I saw that movie," but then later, when they are talking to someone else, they'll say, "No, I haven't seen it."

You seem to be the one who's always having to set the record straight or explain your side of things. The other person is telling little white lies. If one of these signs is present, then there might be some gaslighting going on. Of course, there are always minor misunderstandings between friends and partners; things change over time, and memories are not perfect. But if you are starting to get a sense that your concerns and feelings seem to be getting glossed over, you should talk about it with the other person.

- **Manipulation**

The third sign of gaslighting is that you start to feel like you are being manipulated. You start to think that your feelings are not being taken seriously, even though they are the ones who brought up the subject in the first place. You feel like no matter what you say, and your feelings are dismissed or ignored.

- **Repetitive Behavior**

The fourth sign of gaslighting is that you start to feel like you are being told what to do over and over again. The other person will say things like, "If you don't stop doing that, then I'm never going to believe anything else that you say." They will make it clear that they want something from you repeatedly.

Gaslighting people by repeating requests is unconscious manipulation. If all four signs of gaslighting are present, then there is some gaslighting going on. This can be emotional abuse for women or emotional abuse in a relationship for men.

- **They Never Apologize**

The fifth sign of gaslighting is that the other person never apologizes.

If one of the signs of gaslighting is present, then they are sorry, but you feel like they are sorry solely because you are making them feel guilty.

You will apologize to them repeatedly, hoping that it will make it all better, but nothing seems to change. They assume that you do things wrong and they don't take responsibility for their actions. They don't take accountability or responsibility for anything in their life or theirs.

This should be a red flag if there are any allegations of physical violence within your relationship. This is not normal behavior and should be looked into and dealt with accordingly.

- **Emotional Projection**

The sixth sign of gaslighting is that you start to feel like the other person is projecting their feelings on you. You seem always to be doing something wrong, even though there is plenty of evidence that they are the ones with the problem.

Emotional projection is when someone has a strong feeling about something and doesn't want to recognize it within themselves, so they blamed another person or a group of people.

- **Constant Self-Doubt**

The seventh sign of gaslighting is that you find yourself feeling emotionally unstable. This emotional drain can make it hard to be sure of who you are, and it can take its toll on your self-esteem. You might find yourself being defensive with other people because you assume that they don't trust or believe you too.

- **It Will Wear You Down**

And the last sign of gaslighting is that you will start to feel like you can't even think straight. You don't feel like yourself anymore. You feel a little bit "out of it." You are thinking a lot about your thoughts and not a lot about what's happening around you.

It's like you have trouble concentrating, but not on the task at hand. You aren't interacting with people who matter to you, but instead spending all of your energy worrying about all of the wrong things with this relationship and how it will end up.

Chapter 2:
How Can Gaslighting Affect You?

Loss of Memory

B y now, you all must have understood that when someone is gaslighting you, they alter your perceptions of reality; it's as if they are overwriting your memory with things that never happened. Over some time, it is very natural for every victim to start questioning their every thought, detail, and memory. But most importantly, you are being hurt multiple times. You experience emotional trauma, and this has a direct impact on the hippocampus region of your brain.

This region is responsible for forming memories in the human brain. When you are under stress or a period of prolonged sadness, then the hippocampus starts shrinking, which, in turn, causes memory loss. And this is not only when you are with the gaslighter. Even if you manage to come out of his/her control, emotional abuse often leaves long-term repercussions on the victim in the form of C-PTSD, PTSD, and phobias.

A Constant Feeling of Guilt

Gaslighting and guilt-tripping go hand in hand. One of the primary tactics used by gaslighters is guilt. They manipulate you so that you will feel guilty and sorry for having any feelings at all. As I told you earlier, gaslighting, at its very core, is a tactic used by abusive people to hide their wrongdoings. Similarly, they will create such a situation that they will blame you for everything that they have done. Thus, you will be made the scapegoat in every case, even when you have done nothing wrong. Guilt is something that can separate you from all the beliefs and convictions you have, and this is what the gaslighter will use against you.

Self-Doubt

One of the most widespread effects of gaslighting is that it makes people doubt themselves after a certain point in time. That is how gaslighters gain the upper hand on you; they make you challenge your perception and reality. Since the gaslighters trick you into believing that your account of events did not happen or they are not valid, you

Slowly start doubting everything about yourself. Self-doubt can be paralyzing, and it can even hamper the process of healing. It can delay your recovery even after you have come out of the clutches of the gaslighter. You doubt your traumatic memories, too, so it is straightforward for the victim to go into denial instead of dealing with those horrors. Denial, then, becomes an automatic response for such victims. There are instances where the victim started doubting their diagnosis because they have been repeatedly told that they imagine things, so they think that maybe this time they are making this up in their minds.

It's not so easy to fix or reverse the effects of such an extended period of gaslighting, but it's not entirely impossible at the same time. After a few months of gaslighting, self-doubt can adversely affect your mind and even push you to the brink of depression. You always have this lingering feeling of incompetence that makes you feel suitable for nothing. All of this leads to chronic fatigue. Your self-will is affected, and so is your self-esteem.

Anxiety

Since you are always on the verge of doubting yourself and your decisions, it is very natural for gaslighting victims to feel anxious. You lose your hold on reality and start losing your sanity after a certain point, and this causes anxiety attacks in several people. Some people even start having nightmares because of the emotional trauma they are carrying. Their feelings have been ignored and invalidated for so long that they now doubt their existence. Others also develop suicidal ideation.

All the manipulation that a victim is subjected to at the hands of the gaslighter ultimately impairs their own emotions. As a result, experts say that some victims of gaslighting also show symptoms of obsessive-compulsive disorder. They develop this because the gaslighter had forced them to constantly re-check themselves, which went on for a considerable period before developing OCD.

Loss of Self-Esteem

Whether the gaslighting abused you intentionally or unintentionally, your self-esteem will take a direct hit, and you will increasingly feel disempowered. This happens because the abuser takes away your right to speak up. You are never allowed to speak up about your feelings or ask for what you need. And when the victim gathers up the courage to speak up, the abuser might use their words against them or shut them up using some other covert tactic.

With time, the victim becomes even more submissive and realizes that life is easier if they listen to the abuser and remain quiet. But to feel human, everyone must have their voice. Gaslighting forces you to shut that voice down, and so, you have no other option than to feel powerless.

Moreover, a gaslighter will constantly make you feel as if you are nothing and no one. When the victim is ridiculed to such an extent, they no longer remember who they are after some time. For example, if your boyfriend is a gaslighter and makes fun of your hobbies, the girlfriend often finds it easier to keep the hobby aside than to stand against the gaslighter because it's mostly futile. Somewhere along with all those nasty comments and criticism of the victim, the person loses themselves. They start doing everything according to the preferences of the gaslighter.

Depression

Several gaslighting victims fall prey to depression because the abusers do not stop until they reach the very core of that person and destroy them from within. They rewire your thinking process entirely and make you dependent on them. You start questioning your reactions and even your feelings because the gaslighter told you that you are neurotic or behaving exaggeratedly.

Chapter 3:
The Stages of Gaslighting

Stages of the Relationship

The first meeting of a narcissist and their new partner almost always looks like something out of a movie. The moment explodes with love. Many partners to narcissists remember the early days as perfect. Somehow, this new person in their lives knew what to say and when to say it and swore they had feelings for them beyond anything they'd ever felt. Maybe they blushed during their first early confession of love.

"I know this is crazy," they'll admit, "but I can't deny it. I'm head over heels for you."

This is love-bombing of the Idealization Stage. This stage helps narcissists draw in someone unsure of themselves. A confident partner won't need this much attention from someone new and might find it stifling. However, someone who's recently been hurt has low self-esteem or feels desperate for a partner will swoon at this kind of attention.

The moment we look at these dream encounters realistically, we start to see the cracks. Why would someone want a relationship with a person they don't know? It's because they've sensed that this is a person with whom they can build codependency. They need this person to reassure themselves that they're the soon-to-be-discovered star they want to be, while the new partner can acquiesce their confidence to build up the narcissist's self-worth.

Of course, this doesn't start right away. After a narcissist secures a promise of love or commitment, they can begin to test their boundaries.

It's hard for a narcissist's partner to say what they did the first time. All they know is that the narcissist shifted from deep love to a nagging discomfort. They won't state anything outright. It could be a basic request for food. "I would love some scrambled eggs this morning," for example. Of course! Love to, darling. Their new partner quickly agrees and makes their version of scrambled eggs.

Several things might happen when the partner brings two plates to the table. First, the narcissist might take one bite and pull a face. Second, they might blink in surprise and say, "That's how you do it?" or another comment meant to undermine the effort. Suddenly, their partner finds themselves apologizing for doing nothing wrong; they fulfilled a request. Instead of a thank you, they get a test.

Will they stand up for themselves or work to make the narcissist happy? If the narcissist has chosen the correct partner—and they usually do—then they'll get the latter response. Instead of receiving a plate of eggs on their head for being a jerk, they'll get profuse promises that the next round will be better. The partner will try harder; they'll find a new recipe.

The partner will then probably rationalize the experience. Hey, they like their eggs a certain way. Some people are picky. Personal tastes are hard to punish. In the meantime, they're also trying not to tell themselves that they deserved a thank you and their eggs are delicious. They won't admit that their partner needs to apologize for their comments and walk out the door.

Instead, they work harder to make their partner happy. They were happy before, right? Wrong. The narcissist only presented a happy face to draw their partner in. Now, they can start the Devaluation Phase. After all, their first round of gaslighting their partner worked perfectly.

They've already introduced the false narrative of convincing their partner that their eggs are the problem, not the narcissist's lack of gratitude. That's a small taste of all the comments to come.

As the two of them spend more time together, the narcissist builds on that first disappointment. They'll sometimes look at their partner and ask, "Are you okay? You seem... I don't know... off." Their partner will take this to heart. Maybe they need to add an extra yoga class or therapy session to their regular regime. They wouldn't say those things if they weren't concerned, right?

The false narrative is an essential element to gaslighting. The narcissist wants their partner to feel like they fall short, no matter how hard they try. If they have a great job, the narcissist devalues the job and their role. They might pose questions like, "How can you work at such a terrible place?" or "You know they underpay you, right?" no matter how much the partner likes their job.

One way a narcissist can steer a person's life into codependency is through money. If their partner leaves their job or allows them to decide how to spend their paycheck, they'll go broke and need the narcissist even more. From what I've seen in relationships, financial abuse is a small step away from emotional abuse. Of course, I don't mean that every narcissist uses it, only that it's an easy option.

This all feeds into the narcissist's ability to lie and exaggerate.

Remember that narcissists will stand by a lie no matter what happens. To help build up a false narrative, they'll also exaggerate.

"You can't organize a closet to save your life!" they'll boom. Their partner might scramble to fix the problem, unaware that the narcissist barely noticed their closet and soon felt too exhausted to ask them what the fuss was about. Narcissists use this hyper-focus on small matters to keep their partners emotionally worn down, too physically tired to fight back, and mentally distracted.

This second part of the relationship sees the narcissist become meaner and colder with each passing day. Nothing their victim does seem right, and they will run from one effort to another. No matter what they do, they never get home at the right time, none of their clothing looks good, and they always make the wrong jokes at parties.

All the narcissist's declarations of love are gone and replaced with criticisms and claims that their partner can't do anything, even listening to the narcissist the right way. As a result, the victim's life is now in chaos. Every time they're heading home from work, they feel a gnaw in their stomach, and their thoughts reel.

Will dinner be good enough? I asked them what they wanted, but what if I misheard them? Will they be happy about my progress at work or accuse me of devaluing their job again? Am I too hard on them? I must be. I don't know why I'm so sensitive.

By the time they walk in the door, the victim doesn't know what to expect from their partner. They can almost visually see the eggshells littering the floor and the tiny spaces between them. It's up to the victim to navigate through this impossible set of obstacles without a single misstep.

The tragedy is that the victim's concentrated efforts only make the narcissist work harder to assure them that they're not good enough, mentally unstable, and no longer attractive. The gaslighting feeds off of itself and creates a whirl of chaos that swings both partners around. The victim only feels better when they get the odd kind word. The narcissist loves their constant efforts to be better but despises them for falling for their tricks.

One day, the partner finally snaps. They've caught the narcissist sexting another person while they washed all the dishes. They hold up the phone and point to the message. What the hell is this?

To the victim's shock, their partner merely blinks in confusion. "What are you talking about?" They show it to the narcissist again. Are they seriously denying what's right in front of them?

"I don't know anything about that. I'm not even sure why you're mad."

Their denial floors their partner. There, in that message, are some of the exact sweet words that they got to hear once, a long time ago. Their partner could at least admit that they're flirting with someone else. But, instead, they insist it never happened. They look at the evidence in their partner's hands and realize that they're in a terrible situation.

After that fight, the narcissist's partner gets a moment of kindness. Then, to their shock, the narcissist comes to them looking upset and apologizes.

"You're so wonderful. I hate to think I've hurt your feelings." They kiss their partner like they used to, and the partner gets a rush of that former love. The text message is forgotten, and the two go back to their evening, telling each other everything is fine.

To any outsiders, these two appear as what they are—codependent participants. Neither one is happy, yet no one wants to end the relationship. They both seem to enjoy the rollercoaster of emotions and to get the rush of the high, despite the constant lows.

Finally, the narcissist can no longer look at the ruins of their former love. This feeling of utter disgust is called the Discarding Phase. The victim can see their partner's disinterest on their face, yet something makes them hold on to the hope that things can get better. They loved them once. What did they do to inspire so much passion and romance before? Can they recreate that same dynamic again?

The victim spends their days feeling confused, emotionally ragged, and desperate to fix whatever it is they think they broke. Our poor partner struggles to make their narcissist happy, but their last-ditch efforts to bring back the magic feeds the narcissist's ego, inspiring them to be worse on all fronts, continuing to wear the victim down.

Chapter 4:
Gaslighting in a Relationship

This form of emotional manipulation is often seen in relationships. Unsurprisingly, most victims are women, who are usually more emotionally invested in a relationship. Although gaslighting can affect anyone, it's often seen in romantic relationships because the victim is already predisposed to trust their partner due to the nature of the relationship.

In a typical relationship, there's an ebb and flow of intimacy and independence. In healthy relationships, partners respect each other's needs for space and share their thoughts and feelings. However, with gaslighting in relationships, there is a different power exchange.

The gaslighter acts as though they have no control over their actions. They blame others for their poor decisions and often refuse to acknowledge their efforts. This is one of the most common symptoms of gaslighting.

The gaslighter blames the victim for their problems or mistakes, even when there are clear signs that they are at fault. Instead of admitting responsibility, the gaslighter will blame the victim for things like being too loud, not being quiet enough, or not being accommodating enough to whatever is happening in the relationship. The gaslighter also tends to blame other people surrounding them for their poor decisions and lack of self-control, although these people have nothing to do with their strife.

This gaslighting tactic may be used to make the victim uncomfortable in their home environment. If the victim feels as though they have done something wrong or want to leave the relationship, they are more likely to believe it. This then perpetuates the cycle of abuse and even more gaslighting.

There are two common reactions when someone is being gaslighted: denial and doubt. Gaslighting is difficult for victims because, even with evidence, it can be tough to put together a complete picture of what's happening in their life and why it's happening. The victim doesn't know how or where to start finding out what's wrong with them. One of the best things a victim can do is to ensure that they are getting enough sleep and eating well. These things are crucial to staying grounded and keeping a clear head.

If you're experiencing gaslighting in a relationship, especially if your partner manipulates your thoughts or feelings of fear in any way, you must seek help immediately. If this is happening to you, there's nothing wrong with seeking professional help from someone who can help walk you through what's happening.

The Victim Will Have Trouble Accepting Who They Are

Gaslighting is often used to destabilize the victim's self-confidence and make them believe that their feelings, thoughts, and behaviors are not valid. Unfortunately, victims aren't often aware of how this form of manipulation affects them until later on in the relationship, when it's already too late.

The Gaslighter Makes You Feel You're Going Crazy

Gaslighting can be one of the most challenging things for victims to overcome because it makes them question their reality. Victims will start to feel anxious, depressed, and even fearful. They will often doubt their memories and start to wonder whether or not they're going crazy. Often the gaslighting is so bad that victims believe they see things that aren't there. For example, they may think their partner's appearance has changed or that their partner is doing something out of spite when it isn't the case. This is all part of the gaslighter's plan to get what they want from a relationship and to have complete control over someone else's life.

The best way to recover from gaslighting is to talk about what's going on. People always appreciate the extra attention, and it's important to remember that you can't change the past.

The Victim May Have Trouble Trusting Others

When a gaslighter is involved in a relationship, they will often target the victim's family and friends, catching them in the act of telling how excellent their partner is. This makes the victim feel more isolated and emotional. Gaslighting is one of the quickest ways to break down trust between any two people, as it gets to the core of what people care about.

The gaslighter will begin to do things like accuse their potential partner of cheating or stealing from others or end up spreading rumors with coworkers and relatives without anyone being able to do anything about it.

The victim will feel alone and vulnerable. They may have a hard time forming new relationships or trusting the right people. This is the last thing that victims need after experiencing gaslighting and manipulation in their relationship. The best way to break up the cycle of gaslighting is to reach out for support and help from someone who can guide you through this process with care and compassion.

Chapter 5:
Gaslighting Everywhere

Gaslighting at the Workplace

Gaslighting at the workplace is the popular term for emotional abuse. It is also known as "crazy-making" or being brainwashed by it. The goal of an abuser is to cause a victim to question their feelings, instincts, and sanity.

When you see red flags like lying, deception, veiled threats, or other warning signs of gaslighting - trust your gut. If you feel that your life is being threatened or this person is manipulating you - trust your gut.

During work time, often, it is hard to say just exactly what someone is doing wrong. It is frustrating to see the mistakes that we have made. We may feel like we have been burned by this person and are upset that they are still there and doing their job. Perhaps, you have been tempted to fire them at one point or another, but questioning them in situations like these can lead to a lot of stress and confusion - remember, these people need you.

They want your job, so they will often find any way possible to turn a negative situation into a positive one.

What causes gaslighting at your workplace?

There are some reasons why people would abuse their power at work. Perhaps the person has had a bad experience with their job and feels they are not being respected at work. Maybe they lack self-confidence or are afraid of being judged or feel unattractive.

The most important thing to remember during these types of situations is that these people NEED YOU! They want your job so badly that they will do anything to make you stay put and keep them in the position. That's right: gaslighting can be manipulative, but it is very subtle and difficult to notice at first. It is hard for the victim to believe that this person can do something so evil without being aware of it.

Tips for handling gaslighting at the workplace

We have all felt like the victim of gaslighting at one point or another in our lives but remember: there are ways to cope and deal with it.

1. Say goodbye if they want you to stay

If you feel uncomfortable or threatened, say yes! Say yes that you understand entirely, and then say goodbye. Remember that they need you! This person needs your leniency to keep their job. Just remember to stay calm and take things slow.

2. Don't give in!

Don't fall for their manipulations. They are doing this to push you into doing something, but don't! Do not give in! They will just continue playing with your emotions and try to get you to do the very thing they want you to. So just don't do it! Don't let them make you feel like the victim because that is what they want from you!

3. Ignorance is bliss - stop trying so hard

By all means, stop trying so hard if you feel like something is wrong and everything just seems off. When you stop whining and complaining about the situation, things will start making a lot more sense.

4. Don't let them emotionally blackmail you

Gaslighting is a very clever way of manipulating people into doing their tasks. Gaslighting is all about emotional manipulation and tricking people into doing what they want them to do. Often they will say things like, " See, I told you so." or "You are so intelligent, think of something else!" They want you to think that everything is your fault or that everything was your fault! Don't fall for it because it will just make things worse!

5. Trust your gut!

As we have mentioned before, trust your gut! If you feel like someone is making you do something that they want - don't do it. Even if they tell you that it is in your best interest to follow the instructions, just stop and think about it. Ultimately, trust yourself.

6. Be creative when solving disputes

Gaslighting in the Home

Gaslighting in the home is a very prevalent issue in society today. It is widespread for parents, teachers, and even family members to gaslight and misdirects the child or teenager's behaviors. The person who does this doesn't necessarily mean to do it; it is just that they are incapable of seeing the child's actual behaviors and thinking that these behaviors reflect on them.

Why would any parent ever want to do this? Gaslighting will always mean achieving their ends in any manipulation or game they may enact. They may think that the child is undermining them or the way they deal with things. The parent who does this could be so invested in their idea of how things should be that they refuse to accept any other point of view. It may be that they are fearful of change and are so rigid in how they think has worked for them in the past, which is why they feel it is essential to repress a child's creativity, freedom, or sexuality.

Gaslighting and children can start as early as infancy. So, for instance, when a mother says, "You did not do that!" because she doesn't want to admit her child did something wrong, she is just scratching the surface of gaslighting behavior.

How to handle gaslighting at your home?

Accept the fact that you cannot change someone else behavior, but you can change how you react to it. It is best to talk to a professional who can help you implement strategies to focus on your goals instead of focusing on what others think about you or how they are treating you. Also, remember that your parents want the best for you and love and support for what they do. It is not personal, so don't make it out as such.

Don't be personal

Targets are faced with severe gaslighting when they are too personal about their relationships. Don't make it personal, though; remember that your employer has every right to dismiss you from your job or reduce your salary - it's their business, after all, and ultimately they will run things in their way. However, this is not necessarily gaslighting as long as there is no element of manipulation involved from their end.

Never give up on someone

A gaslight victim is usually highly challenging; often, they have their demons to battle and little to no support from those supposed to be on their side. As a result, they are frequently exhausted, mentally drained, and impossibly angry - but don't give up on them. Instead, help them along the way by giving them a shoulder to cry on or friends who can talk things out with them or even listen to what they have to say.

Keep the truth at the forefront

Gaslighting is a destructive behavior that can lead to the victim being completely broken. Sadly, so many victims of this abuse end up losing all hope and trust in their partners or friends, often ending up leaving relationships or friendships altogether. To stop this vicious cycle, you must remind them of truth now and again - don't overdo it, though, as this could be a form of manipulation from your end. Instead, remind them of the good things they have in their lives at regular intervals so that they know they have something to fight for.

Remain objective

It's easy to get angry when someone you love is going through gaslighting. The best support I can give is to encourage her to seek help. Unfortunately, people with this disorder cannot be helped, and the person who is suffocating will go through gaslighting to the point of getting herself emotionally (and perhaps physically) harmed. The only thing I can do is try to help her break free from it. That's the least I can do, and it makes me feel a little better.

Gaslighting in the Society

Gaslighting is a socially acceptable way for people to manipulate others for their ends. In the past, it was better to gaslight others than it is today. This is because there has been a shift in the social climate that makes this behavior unacceptable and even illegal - although it still occurs every day.

Examples of gaslighting in society are when you witness someone claiming that something that happened didn't happen at all. Or when someone says something and has you believing it happened in a certain way, but then you later realize that it didn't happen at all. Many people who do things like this use gaslighting to get what they want or manipulate others for their own gain. These types of behavior can be morally wrong and will affect how other people around you view you too.

Toxic Society

If you have read the definition of gaslighting above, then you will understand that gaslighting is a pretty major issue with society in general. This is because the gap between what is acceptable and what is not permitted to do has become very large, affecting how other people around you view everything in this world. As a result, some things are upsets for some people, while others are just minor issues or even no issues.

These factors lead to this rise in gaslighting, which happens due to:

- Too many issues today that people are sensitive about
- People who want or need attention from their friends and family

These are all factors that affect how hard it is for a person to tell the truth. How they see you may not be how you see them at all.

Tips on how to handle gaslighting on the society

1. Don't take offense when you are treated poorly

For some reason, people often feel the need to make a person they dislike or have an issue with feeling offended. It's not because they want you to feel bad about yourself or make you feel like crap. It's because they want to show how much of a victim they are and how they can have a problem with others who have power over them.

2. Be honest

Just be honest with yourself and speak your true feelings and opinions. It may hurt, but it is the only thing that will eventually help someone and help them realize that you are not bothering them much at all. Be nice about it, though and don't make it seem like something you want to do; instead, do it because you wish to help them.

3. Avoid negative situations

Just try to avoid the situation altogether if possible. If not, then be careful who you are around and what you say or do so that you don't get involved in a situation where gaslighting might be a factor. It's not always easy to avoid, but people should try if they don't want to get caught up in drama or games where gaslighting is commonplace.

Gaslighting is a prevalent form of emotional abuse and more confusing because the abuser has no desire to cause harm. As a result, the victim ends up questioning themselves, their sanity, and their reality.

Gaslighting through Technology

When abused through technology, the first thing a person should do is confront their abuser. This can be done in person, over the phone, or through social media sites. If this doesn't work, then a restraining order might need to be issued so that the abuser can't contact them electronically anymore. This might seem extreme, but it sometimes needs to happen for the victim to move on with their life and not feel as though their abuser is constantly attacking them.

Society vs. Social Media

There is some definite difference between the two that the victim needs to understand regarding gaslighting, society versus social media. Society involves a group of people who know each other and have been friends for a while. These people are primarily similar personalities and have similar issues. Social media doesn't have a set group of people or anything called "society." Social media works because the person or persons create a profile on it, explaining who they are and what they are about. Then they are contacted by many different people worldwide because of these profiles showing up on search result pages.

The way gaslighting on social media works is that the abuser has already been a friend of the victim and has gotten to know each other pretty well. Therefore, the abuser knows what buttons to press to make the victim feel like they are doing something wrong. This works because the abuser will create a fake profile using the person's real name, but they will change their picture and description completely, so it sounds as if it is coming from a completely different person. The victim then believes what this fake profile says about them and frequently gets angered because of how they are being treated (through the fake profile).

For example, a person may be getting emotionally abused at work and feel that they can't talk to anyone about it - so they create a fake profile on social media that looks different from their real personality. They make up a complete profile of their character and then set it up so that the shape will pop up instead of the natural person's name when someone searches for their name. This is done because the abuser wants to have all of the power in the situation, which would be impossible if they were being talked to one-on-one by the victim.

To stop gaslighting from happening, the victim needs to confront their abuser and ask them why they are doing this. Then, they need to explain what will show them that they realize what is happening and do not want that relationship anymore. Finally, for things like this to stop completely, the victim needs to get out of the relationship entirely or make the abuser promise never again to do what they did in the first place.

How to handle gaslighting on social media?

To help stop gaslighting from happening, you need to confront the abuser and ask them why they are doing this. When confronting your abuser, be prepared for them to defend themselves and their actions. You need to be sure that you have facts and evidence to prove that what they are saying is wrong.

They may try to lie about everything and blame it all on something else. They will try to make it look like they are the victims in everything and want you to think that everything is okay. To prove that they are being gaslighted, talk with other people who have been in a similar situation as you have been in before. Ask what made them realize what was going on and if there were any good ways of dealing with things after the gaslighting was over.

There are people out there who can help you and support you through anything, so don't be afraid to ask for their help - all they want is for things to be better for everyone involved.

Chapter 6:
Things Narcissists Say During Gaslighting

Gaslighting can be physically abusive as well as destructive emotionally; it is prevalent in abusive relationships. It's been widely debated whether or not borderline personalities are susceptible to gaslighting. Still, the following list of statements was compiled from various sources and examples found on the internet, which covers a wide range of personality types.

When you are with a narcissist, there is a sense that they can control your world. They can make you believe things that don't exist, making you question your sanity. It is called gaslighting, or "the narc-game," for a good reason.

Here are the 100 things narcissists say during gaslighting that your friends will not tell you.

This is open to anyone who believes they may be in a relationship with a narcissist or diagnosed with a borderline personality disorder. You have the right to decide what is best for you, and only you can do that.

1. "You are over-reacting."
1. "The victim is hypersensitive and over-emotional."
2. "Why do you have to make everything so dramatic? It is not that bad. I am 100% honest with you."
3. "Just relax. I am just joking around."
4. "I am sorry I hurt your feelings like that before, but that does not mean I still don't love you.."

5. "I don't know what your deal is, but can you just grow up already?"

6. "It is just a misunderstanding."

7. "Are you jealous of _____? I thought we were best friends?" (regarding another female at your expense)

8. "I am just trying to help you."

9. "Why don't you ever trust me?"

10. "I am just kidding around with you. Lighten up."

11. "I am not upset; why are you upset?"

12. "I said I was sorry. What else do you want from me?"

13. "You're ridiculous."

14. "We will talk about this later."

15. "I just want to help my friend, what is wrong with that?" (regarding another female at your expense)

16. "You are so insensitive."

17. "I never said that."

18. "I was not lying to you if I look up the definition of _____, a liar is someone who purposefully misleads another person for their benefit. I never misled you on purpose!" (When they are misleading you.)

19. "You promised me already."

20. "It's not my fault that he/she left me!"

21. "There is nothing wrong with me." (When there is something wrong with them. This is an excuse to avoid treatment or help.)

22. "I didn't lie, and I just left out some minor details."

23. "You should be happy I am in a relationship with you... You are so lucky."

24. "My life was perfect before you came into it." (When your existence is ruining their life and they are making it clear that they want little to nothing to do with you.)

25. "You are thinking about it the wrong way." (When the narc knows that they are deceiving you, but since they have convinced themselves that what they say is true, then anyone who is questioning them must be wrong.)

26. "Oh, that's nothing. Less than nothing." (When something is wrong with them and they know it.)

27. "My life is perfect now. I am happy." (When they are doing just the opposite; narcissists will show you no proof that their lives are great by the way they treat others or present themselves when around you, but since they believe it, they are showing that their lives are lovely.)

28. "I don't know what my problem was before we met."

29. "I always want to make you happy.."

30. "I promise I will never do it again."

31. "You don't have to feel bad about this...It has nothing to do with you."

32. "I never lied to you. I just didn't tell you the full story."

33. "You are so weird right now!" (When they completely lose their cool over something trivial.)

34. "You never trust me." (When they have shown that it is tough for them to be trustworthy, even when they say they will do something, it is usually not done as promised.)

35. "I'm sorry. I should have done that differently."

36. "You are still acting as he/she cheated on you." (This means the narc does not have any faith in themselves, so they

need to keep telling others that they believe this accusation of theirs is true.)

37. "Stop thinking about it!"

38. "Think about what happened, and then tell me what to do."

39. "Maybe you are right...Maybe there is something wrong with you. I'm sorry." (When there is no way you are right or that there is something wrong with you, the narc just wants to make you feel like there is something wrong with you for picking up on the sick, dehumanizing way they interact with others.)

40. "It's not my fault that I get upset over this."

41. "I didn't do it on purpose." (This excuse is used when your narcissist did not have any control over their actions and didn't want to take responsibility for the hurtful things they did.)

42. "I am a victim. You're the one that is crazy." (When the narcissist continues to tell others about how they were "victimized" by the situation, it is usually because they are lying to themselves and feel as if they did something wrong.)

43. "I am sorry. I shouldn't have done that (or said those things)."

44. "You'll always have a place in my heart." (A narcissist cannot take responsibility for their actions, so they tell you that you will be with them forever, even if you leave them.)

45. "I didn't mean it like that!" (The narcissist can never admit when they have been utterly wrong about something. They

have to find another way of putting a spin on the situation and having you feel bad.)

46. "You know I didn't mean it!"

47. "I would not hurt you for the world. You know I love you!"

48. "What are you so upset about? It's not that big of a deal." (A narcissist will tell others that everything is okay when in reality, they were appalled at someone.)

49. "I'm sorry. I made a mistake."

50. "Today is a new day." (This is something that will be said when the Narcissist has done something awful and wants to move on with life.)

51. "I know I have been acting a little strange lately. It means nothing against you."

52. "If I did it, it does not mean anything."

53. "You are jealous of me!"

54. "You are very insecure and need to get over yourself."

55. "I will never change." (The narcissist has no intentions of changing for the better in your eyes.)

56. "Nothing is ever good enough for you." (The narcissist expects perfection and is upset when they do not receive it.)

57. "You're a great guy, but I just don't love you anymore. It's just not the same." (The narcissist uses a form of displacement: "You're great guy, but I just don't love you anymore. It's just not the same." This way, they don't have to own their feelings and their behavior.)

58. "I'm sorry, but I know this hurts you, and I can see how upset you are. But it's over - I'm leaving." (The narcissist

is sorry that this hurts them - they are angry that their control is being challenged.)

59. "I know you're thinking about how mean and cruel I was to leave you like this when we've been together for so long. But that is not it at all. It has nothing to do with you. You're just dramatic."

60. "You and I are just not a good match."

61. "You are so bossy."

62. "It's your fault I'm like this." (The narcissist is always right even when they aren't.)

63. "Don't be angry, and it's not worth it!" (This is said when the Narcissist does something awful and doesn't want to acknowledge that their behavior was terrible)

64. "Just calm down!" (The narcissist says this immediately before pushing you, yelling at you, or attacking you.)

65. "I know you like doing that, so I'll make it easy for you: You're out!" (The narcissist says this before kicking you out of the relationship.)

66. "You're just not good enough for me." (The narcissist does not want anything to do with anyone but themselves.)

67. "If I loved you, do you think I would let things get as bad as they have?" (This is said when the Narcissist can't be bothered to be honest with you about how they feel.)

68. "You've become so cynical about me." (This is said when you question the narcissist's behavior, and often you haven't been cynical at all but concerned.)

69. "I am trying to be happy again!" (Conveniently leaving out that you were unhappy before meeting up with someone else.)

70. "It is not my fault that we have to break up... he/she is a cheater." (The narcissist will use this to try and manipulate someone else into leaving you. They will not take responsibility for their actions.)

71. "You are so hard on me." (This is said when the narcissist has made a mistake or done something wrong and doesn't want to own it.)

72. "It's not that bad...If you can get over it, then I can too." (The narcissist is trying to convince others that their behavior was okay as long as they can get over the situation, but unless you also agree to participate in the Narcissists game, then your old behaviors are not acceptable by them too.)

73. "Do you think I care what he/she thinks?" (The narcissist is trying to make others think that they don't care what other people think when the truth is that they do manage and can't handle criticism from others.)

74. "I'm not going to be your doormat." (The narcissist says this when you ask them where they were when they made plans with you and then cancel on you.)

75. "I don't want to hurt you, but... " (The narcissist is trying to manipulate your feelings. The Narcissist will not take responsibility for their actions and can't take the criticism.)

76. "I wouldn't do that to you." (The narcissist says this when they are lying and make you think they are honest when they know exactly what they are doing.)

77. "You look so stressed!" (The narcissist does not want anything negative to happen around them and sees it as a problem when someone else is stressed or upset.)

78. "I am sorry I made you feel that way too. I know it is not your fault." (The narcissist cares about how they make others feel, but they are not willing to take responsibility for what they have done. They will try to empathize with you, but they aren't ready to change their behaviors in any way.)

79. "How can you be so angry at me?" (The narcissist says this when you are upset by the way they have treated you.)

80. "Don't worry about me." (The narcissist says this the instant that you are worried about them and don't want to do anything that may hurt them.)

81. "You should be happy that I am still around."

82. "Don't be so dramatic." (The narcissist is always right and will tell others that their feelings are wrong.)

83. "I don't care what you think." (The narcissists will say this when they have gone out of their way not to say anything wrong about someone else or hurt their feelings but are willing to throw you under the bus.)

84. "I am not feeling well today... I'm sorry if it shows. It's nothing serious." (The narcissist is unwilling to take responsibility for their actions but will tell others that they are sick. This is a way to manipulate others into thinking that they are ill and not worth it.)

85. "I know I have been acting strange lately, but it means nothing against you."

86. "I'll be fine in a minute."

87. "You're too sensitive!" (This is said by the narcissist when you begin to express concern about them.)

88. "I'm sorry I always do this to you! You're so jealous!"

89. "You're paranoid - it's not like that at all!" (The narcissist will tell others that they are overreacting and having an irrational reaction due to their faults but has no intention of changing.)

90. "You know I wouldn't do anything like that on purpose. I didn't mean to hurt your feelings."

Chapter 7:
Why Narcissists Prey on Intelligent People

J ust because you are aware of the person in your life who is abusing you and aware of their true nature does not mean it will be easy to sever the tie. Intelligent people will constantly be able to peg the narcissist for who they indeed are and what they are doing to cause damage to their partner, but that does not mean the victim will be able to figure out how to leave the situation. This is one of the biggest problems that intelligent people in a selfish situation will face.

It has been shown repeatedly that intelligent people are the most susceptible to being taken advantage of by a narcissist. On the surface, a narcissist will target someone because of their attributes. They look for loving and giving people to try and take advantage of them. When you are a giving person, the narcissist will adore you because they are focused on taking. When you are intelligent, you also offer better levels of stimulus to the narcissist.

Intelligent people are also better at cleaning up the messes that narcissists make in their lives. Smart people tend to have the ability to achieve goals and think things through to find solutions. This is very drawing to the narcissist. They want to take advantage of your intelligence and use it for their good.

Equally as important in knowing why the narcissist chooses you is why you are selecting the narcissist. Looking at ourselves and trying to understand why we have decided to enter into a relationship with a narcissist can give us clues that help us better understand ourselves.

With this understanding, it is easier to regain control over your own life instead of leaving it in the hands of your narcissistic abuser.

Intelligent people tend to rely on their rational brains to make decisions instead of trusting their instincts and gut feelings. As a result, they tend not to follow the suggestions that their inner surfaces are laying out. Instead, intelligent people are more apt to disregard their feelings and listen to the story being played in their minds.

One of the main problems relying on your conscious mind is that it is only a fraction of what helps us make decisions in life. Our past experiences are also going to play a role. We learn, and our decisions are based on the things we know; however, we also fall into patterns. Childhood traumas or other life events can dictate these patterns. They can steer us in the entirely wrong direction and into the arms of a narcissist.

Intelligent people are also extremely well-versed in figuring out ways to justify just about anything. These elaborate or straightforward justifications are used to quiet the inner voice that is trying to warn us that something is about to go wrong. It is unfortunate, but we usually go to the justification rather than adjusting our path and listening to our inner voice.

An excellent example of this will be if you are on a second or third date with a person. While sitting at the table, you notice that the person you are on a date with keeps glancing at other people. Your inner voice sends you a warning that they are not as into you are. But, unfortunately, you are them, and they are still on the lookout for a suitable mate.

It is sending you warning signs that the person you are on a date with may be deceitful or end up being a cheater. However, rather than paying attention to these warning signs and taking a step back, you justify their actions by thinking things like, "Maybe they weren't looking at other people," or "What is the harm in gazing at others? I can appreciate when someone is attractive too without being a cheater." These justifications are common, and they can lead to disaster. When your inner self recognizes red flags, you must pay attention to them; they can help keep you safe from narcissistic abuse and other toxic relationships.

Intelligent people also tend to think that they can handle anything that life has to throw at them. You can become wrapped up in it so quickly that you are unable to think straight regardless of if you are intelligent or not. So, listening to your gut feelings about someone is one of the best ways to stay safe, and having an understanding that you shouldn't have to try and handle the outrageous nature of a narcissist is also advantageous.

Narcissists love to prey on intelligent people because they are a bit more of a challenge. However, you must remember that the narcissist is playing a game, and they hope you don't realize it. They like to take control, and beating an intelligent person into submission is more fulfilling to their nefarious ways.

They find more joy in dragging an intelligent person down because it helps to prove that they are superior to everyone. Narcissists draw intelligent people in a variety of ways. More often than not, the narcissist is going to be exceptionally charming and charismatic. They are frequently well versed in academic subjects that helps draw intelligent people in. It is easy to become enthralled with the narcissist as they showboat and make themselves look great.

Recognizing their lies can be insanely hard because they have become so good at it.

Relationships with narcissists often start like normal relationships. They allow you to get comfortable and fall for them before they turn the table to take total control over you and your life. However, it can take a considerable amount of time before they will flip the script and start to take advantage of you. They may build you up in the beginning and look as if they are a safe and trusting support network for you, and then they will start to tear down your walls and abuse you in every way possible.

Intelligent people also tend to be more reliable than others. They will go to great lengths to fulfill their promises, even if they promise that goes against their typical beliefs. Narcissists will prey on this fact and try to get you to agree to many different things, knowing you will stand by your word.

There is also the issue of dedication. When you are intelligent, you typically have a higher level of dedication to all things you feel are essential. They want to give their whole self to it and, in turn, expect that their partner is doing the same. The narcissist knows this and will allow you to think that they are all-in, just like you. They will then take advantage of your dedication to them, knowing you will go to great lengths to make sure you stay together and that you are a united front. What will slip by the intelligent person is the fact that only one person is in control here, the narcissist, and only one person is dedicated to the relationship, the victim, or in this case, you.

Another factor that plays into why narcissists prey on intelligent people is that smart people tend to be perfectionists. They want to do their best in every situation, and they will work very hard to accomplish tasks so that they receive an acknowledgment.

The narcissist will set you up for failure every time they want you to believe you can't do anything right. They know you will continue to strive for perfection. No matter how hard you try, you must understand that nothing you can do to make the narcissist in your life gives you the acknowledgment you deserve. They will continue to beat you down and make you feel as if you can do nothing right so that you will keep trying, and they can maintain control of the situation and you.

Intelligent people also tend to have a good work ethic and some amount of personal accountability. This means they can admit when they are wrong or if they mess up. The narcissist will prey on this by twisting situations so the victim always looks like they are in the wrong. When a person is wired to have accountability, and then life situations are twisted, they are more apt to accept blame even if they don't deserve it.

Intellect can help you in various ways; however, it is crucial to understand that simply being intelligent does not mean you will always make good decisions. Intelligent people are more apt to make destructive decisions because they are better at making up excuses to justify why the decision will not be dangerous.

Getting the thoughts and ideas from a trusted person on just about any problem can help you gain insight and various perspectives, which can help lead you to better decision making and less justification to make poor decisions.

Chapter 8:
How to Handle the Effects of Gaslighting

G aslighting is a manipulative tool that abusers use to confuse and entrap their victims. It's hard to free yourself from the grip of gaslighting because these abusers isolate their victims then cut them off from reality.

Gaslighting can be subtle or overt and is often mistaken for the "normal" ups and downs of a relationship. When you are being gaslighted, you might be so confused by the outlandish lies that you doubt your sanity. You may also feel guilty, or like you did something to provoke such treatment.

If you have been gaslit before or feel like you are gaslit, know that it is never too late to start again. Keep a journal detailing your conversations and emotions. This can help with sanity checks on what's happening in your relationship.

Know that the manipulation is designed to make you question your reality and trust. Know that it is designed to make your uncertainty grow and become confused to become more dependent on the person gaslighting you.

Remember, this is not a person you are trying to get back with and start over again with, but an abuser who is doing everything in his power to keep his power trip going. He's not doing anything wrong intentionally, and he does what he does because he can. Remember that he doesn't care about you; he only cares about himself. Trust yourself enough to leave him and find yourself again.

Don't forget to take care of yourself by eating right, getting regular exercise and sleep, and keeping up with your hobbies. Remember that you shouldn't try to do anything that requires much concentration or thought if your head is not clear from all the years of abuse and mind games. Stay away from any people who tell you what you should or shouldn't be doing or feeling because they are trying to get inside your head again. Instead, start doing things that bring you happiness.

Remember to be gentle with yourself when the gaslighting kicks in. No one can make you doubt your own ability to take care of yourself. Instead, stand up for yourself and continue believing in yourself. You are going to be okay, even if it doesn't seem like it right now.

Know that you don't have to do anything that makes you uncomfortable, even if someone tells you otherwise. You can leave, tell them no, or firmly stand your ground. Make decisions based on your feelings and what feels right to you. Trust your gut instinct over anything else, but especially when it comes to yourself and what's best for you.

Stop taking things personally and know that the gaslighting behavior isn't about YOU. Abusers thrive on making their victims feel small and worthless to control them and keep them trapped. Abusers will find any way to manage their victims and will get away with anything if you let them.

Don't get caught up in your head. When you are gaslight, it is tough to keep your cool, but that's the only way you will do well in recovering from gaslighting by not giving in to the confusion and believing that it's somehow your fault or something you have done. Try not to blame yourself for what someone has said or done because you may have misinterpreted it; take a good look at all the elements of what happened before making a big deal out of it.

Never follow an abuser's orders; always stand your ground no matter what because a gaslighting abuser doesn't care about what's best for you. He just wants to keep getting his gaslighting in and out of your life. And although he might believe he is justified in using force even though the law says otherwise, he is wrong, and you should definitely stand up for yourself and fight back if necessary. Fight back against any thoughts or feelings that tell you that something is wrong with being who you are. Always trust in yourself and know that there is nothing wrong with being who you are or doing what makes you happy.

Don't give up on yourself; you can make it through this and will be stronger for it. Never give up on yourself or your good judgment just because someone tells you, "You're nothing" and "You're crazy." Remember that all abusers say that their victim is crazy; don't let them define who you are.

If a person gaslights you, it means they have told you repeatedly that they are better than you. Your self-esteem is undermined that you don't even think you are worth anything anymore. You will always please them and give them what they want, but they will find any reason to tell you not to do it. They will tell you things like, "You're stupid." "You're worthless." "I'm right; I'm better than you." This is all gaslighting, so don't let them get away with it!

It is believed that gaslighting comes from a culture in which women have been second-class citizens for centuries. Gaslighting means that you have been tricked into thinking that the person who gaslights you is more important than it is. It's like they have tricked you into doubting yourself and your intelligence and feelings. It's a way to undermine your self-confidence, make you second guess everything, make you think that everything is wrong with you, and make your mind distrust itself so that it doubts all your thoughts.

It can come in many forms, so there will be many ways of explaining what it means to be gaslighted. For example, a gaslighter might use these different ways to undermine a person:

- They try to "hide the truth." Maybe they will throw out some false information, which they know is incorrect, and it's just to confuse you. Or they will say something that contradicts what you're saying and then tell you that you must be wrong. They might also say something, like how beautiful the setting is at night, that throws your mind off track and makes you think about whether or not it's so beautiful. That is gaslighting because they are doing it on purpose to get your mind off of them and try to make you doubt yourself.

- They try to create a sense of false fairness. Sometimes, a gaslighter will act like they are giving you something of value when really, it's a setup. For example, they'll smile and say, "I'm going to give you this necklace just because I want to." Then, later on in the evening, when you wear the necklace out somewhere, you'll see them looking at it and trying to reach out and grab it subtly. That's gaslighting because what they did was an attempt to gain something from the generosity they had given for free earlier.

- They try to say that what happened didn't happen.

- They try to make you think that what happened was your fault.

- They tell you that it's your fault they want what they have through some manipulation, such as saying the wrong thing at just the right time or making you look bad by being around when you have something you shouldn't be having, like taking a day off work or gossiping with someone about their love life.

- They tell lies to keep things moving forward so that they won't look bad in front of people. Usually, it's not intentional lies but misleading statements that come from desperation to keep things going because they can't let go and move on.

- They make you second guess yourself by giving you the evil eye, putting you down, or staring at you.

- They pretend that they are your friend when they want something from you. Of course, it's not that simple in most cases, but often it starts down that path and becomes twisted into something more weird and unrecognizable.

- They start as a perfect guy who seems genuine and caring at first so that later on, they can do whatever they want to you.

Usually, the gaslighter is someone who is very insecure and doesn't have self-esteem or confidence of any sort. They have low self-esteem, and it causes them to go out trying to replace their lack of self-worth with someone or something else. Usually, they start as a nice person and seem supposedly loving and caring towards you. Still, then you see how they are so controlling and abusive behind the scenes that it seems like a stalker is following you in your own life.

Chapter 9:
Powerful Ways to Disarm a Gaslighter

Sometimes, you cannot just pick up your things and walk out on a gaslighter. They may be your benefactor, or you may be married to them and have children with them; and now you are scared of having your kids go through the trauma of a parent's divorce. It could also be that you are gainfully employed somewhere, and your gaslighting is of the workplace type. Finally, sometimes, you cannot simply walk away because you love the gaslighter so much, and you believe that they can change. Several scenarios might make it difficult just to break free from a gaslighter. In that case, the best option available to you is to disarm the gaslighter. Here we will explain some techniques of the first stage of fighting back: disarming the gaslighter, removing their tools, and putting up the first line of defense.

If you have to contact a gaslighter, it's essential to minimize the damage they can do to you and even avoid that damage altogether.

Keep a Log of Events and Conversations

Having written, material evidence of what happened can help take away some power from the gaslighter. They will try to deny it all anyway, but if you make it a practice, they may realize that it will be harder to get to you

Since gaslighters thrive on denying and lying, having a witness to your conversations with them can also be helpful. An outsider (a co-worker, another family member, etc.) can later vouch for one of you. If the gaslighter denies and lies, you will have someone validate your claims and keep you grounded. Validating your claim might be all you need, no doubt your reasoning. Since the gaslighter is out to make you believe that you imagine things, having someone else think your version/reality will make it harder for the gaslighter to convince you that you imagine things.

It will be more challenging in relationships, as a lot of the gaslighting happens in private. In that case, there might not be a third party to serve as a witness when there is a denial.

Stand up for your Feelings

To disarm a gaslighter, you need to stand up for your emotions and yourself. But you need first to remember what and how you feel. Victims that have suffered from prolonged gaslighting often stop listening to their voice since they're always criticized. Meditation, journaling, and other mindful activities can help you get back to having your thoughts and being confident of them

Avoid Direction Confrontation

One of how the gaslighter will react is blame-shifting. Because they're often inclined to project, they may try to turn the table and cast the same accusation on you if you accuse them of gaslighting; or they may resort to personal attacks.

Name What's Happening

Giving the issue a name makes it more "tangible" and manageable. Make sure you call what's happening "gaslighting," at least to yourself. It can be helpful to also call it out loud to others. When you identify what is going on, you become aware of the pattern of undermining behavior. So, when the gaslighter uses its tactics on you, you can immediately recognize it for what it is and shrug it off immediately.

Rebuild Your Self-Esteem

Work on rebuilding your self-esteem. The gaslighter will try to make it seem like you are an unlovable person, but you mustn't allow that. The opinion of the gaslighter is just one in thousands of people that know you, and I'm sure you have other people around you that love you for who you are. You can quickly grow your self-esteem by reminding yourself of the time before you met the gaslighter—when you felt safe, secured, loved, and safe. So, if you don't feel good about yourself now, then it has everything to do with the gaslighter and not with you. If it is difficult for you to recall those good times, maybe due to the level of damage that the gaslighter has done, you may opt to remember you're positive memories gradually and write them down in your journal.

Check to See If Your Conversations are Power Struggles

How do you know if it is a power struggle? When you notice that the person you are dealing with is attempting to gain the upper hand and prove that they are correct and that you are wrong. If you are not careful, you too will be struggling to get the approval of the gaslighter to get them to see the situation the way you see it; but then we know that is never going to happen.

A power struggle is different from a real conversation. In a real conversation, there is no battle for who is right or wrong. Instead, you and your partner are more concerned with listening to each other's concerns, and your primary concern is to sort things out amicably so that both of you leave the conversation feeling heard. Anything different from this is a power struggle, and you know better than to get into a power struggle with a gaslighter because you will never win. Instead, you will experience the gaslighting effect some more.

Gaslighters thrive more when you engage with them. They want you both to go on with the back-and-forth conversations about who is right and who is not. Don't give them that chance. Simply don't engage with them. To them, it is like a game, and they need somebody to play it with. You can stay with them and choose not to play the game. If you do that, you won't be sucked into the manipulation. Instead of going on with the power struggle, recognize it for what it is, and tell the gaslighter that you don't want to proceed with the conversation.

Call Them Out

A confrontation is never an option when disarming a gaslighter because things can go sideways. But you have a better choice than confrontation, and it is calling them out. You can let the gaslighter know that you know what they are trying to do to you. Tell them that you are not willing to partake in this relationship and that you want it to stop. This will deflate their ego and disarm them because they know that you are aware of all their subtle manipulations. It would be stupid of them to try and manipulate you ever again.

Sort Out Truth from Distortion

When you are dealing with a gaslighter, be prepared to hear different versions of any given event, an act that is meant to confuse you. They are masters at this, so they will include some truths in what they say to get you to believe the whole story. Clarify your thinking and sort out the fact from the lies. It is not a difficult thing. You just have to look at the two sides of what they tell you. They will always be the real thing and something else that they want you to believe. For instance, they may say that you are overreacting to something that is not worth this amount of attention. But then you know within you that the issue is worth the attention you are giving it. Now you have identified the distortion which is aimed at making you look crazy.

Hold on to What You Know is True

Lies, deceits, and manipulation characterize gaslighting, but you can disarm your gaslighter if you hold on to the things you know are true. You may have been lied to before, but you can carefully pick out the truths and hold on to them, rain or come shine. Doing this will eliminate the seeds of self-doubt that the gaslighter is doing everything to plant into you. And when you refuse to permit self-doubt, you are better equipped to see the schemes being plotted by the gaslighter.

Identify the Gaslight Triggers

When you are involved with a gaslighter, there will always be certain things that trigger the gaslighting process. You can take some time and look over all the instances your gaslighter has tried to manipulate you and see the main issues that led to it. Once you identify those triggers, you can avoid them altogether, or you avoid talking about those things with them. The catalysts may fall into broad categories, which include certain situations, topics, words. Some examples are money, sex, children, cheating, and inheritance, among others.

If your instinct is avoiding them, then you should make conscious efforts to avoid them altogether.

1. When a gaslighter wants to accuse you, they will attach a little truth to their lie and go on to blow it out of proportion. This is done to leave you wondering if they are right or wrong. And it can be hard deciding this because there will be some form of truth to it, making it difficult for you to determine if they are right or just manipulating you.

Let me illustrate with an example. Let's say that you and your gaslighting partner attend a party and meet up with an old friend. Because it's been a while, you get caught up in the moment and spend a reasonable amount of time with your friend. Your partner might conclude that you were flirting and that you did it intentionally to humiliate them. Now, you can't say for sure if that is what it seems like. You may become confused at the moment, but you know deep down that all you did was communicate freely with a long-lost friend.

The best way to proceed in such a case is to check your feelings rather than decide if they are right or wrong. If by narrowing your feelings, you discover that you are guilty of what you are being accused of and you feel remorse, you can apologize. But if you feel attacked or bewildered, that means you are being gaslighted, and the best way to proceed is to disengage immediately.

2. Realize that you can't control their opinion. Some victims of gaslighting remain victims for so long because they erroneously believe that they can change the opinion of the gaslighter. But we know that this might never happen. So rather than trying to change their opinion, choose freedom instead. Let me give you a scenario. If your partner is doing

something that you know for sure is not correct (like consuming too much alcohol), and you are busy trying to make them see reasons with you.

You can see that this situation could have been avoided if you hadn't tried to change their opinion about alcohol. But, unfortunately, no matter what you tell them about the effects of excessive alcoholism, a gaslighter will always hold on to their views on alcoholism. So, if you know that trying to change them will only gaslight you further, then you need to let it be.

Chapter 10:
Gaslighting Repellent: How to Shut Down a Narcissist

N arcissists don't process or experience feelings of how healthy individuals do, which is reflected in their detrimental conduct. You can't react to a narcissist in the way you may respond to other individuals and anticipate a comparable result. The narcissist sees their behavior as ordinary. They control, exploit, and carry around a misrepresented sense of self-importance that makes them genuinely believe that they are generally morally justified. Every other person is the issue. Due to this and many of their numerous character issues and psychological maladjustments, the narcissist leaves casualties of destroying maltreatment in their wake.

When a narcissist says something critical about a vulnerability of yours, it puts you into a mode of defense, you feel threatened, and you can't think through the solution to the problem at hand.

Entering defense mode, psychologists say, comes from the need to protect ourselves when we face a threatening situation. The rational part of the brain is shut in this mode, and only our survival matters.

It is not often necessary to enter defense mode in our relations with others, but the narcissist is always self-absorbed as they seek to fulfill only their own needs always. Therefore, narcissists are always in defense mode and will attempt to put the people around them in this mode, which results in two people who are too occupied with protecting themselves instead of logically tackling a problem.

Here you will identify the ones the narcissist has been exploiting to make you think you are crazy:

Abandonment. This is a familiar feeling that the people in your life will not be there for you. You feel you can't count on your parents, your siblings, or people close to you for emotional support. It is a feeling of fear that the critical people in your life will leave you.

Abandonment can be a form of anxiety, and the loss of people is a characteristic of life, whether it is the end of a relationship or the passing on of a loved one. Be that as it may, individuals with abandonment issues live in dread of losing people. They may likewise unintentionally do things that push individuals to leave, so they're never surprised when people go them.

A fear of abandonment isn't a recognized condition in mental health, per se. Instead, it's considered a type of fear and is treated as such. Some indicators of this kind of vulnerability are:

- You feel your parents won't be there when you need them.
- You feel your siblings or close friends won't be there for you.
- You continuously need assurance from friends and loved ones, and you urge them to make statements like "I will always be there for you."

Shame. This is a psychological feeling of inadequateness, that you are not good enough or inferior to others, that others won't love who you are and will always reject you. Shame has to do with the negative feelings we have about ourselves, triggered whenever we are disappointed or when we get tested by a challenging situation.

Shame is one of the most dominant feelings that we feel as humans. It can make us cut off social connections, fuel our addictions, and sink us into a pit of depression. It might even lead to suicide in some cases.

For many individuals, shame is a feeling they feel to a shifting degree consistently. How do you recognize this kind of vulnerability?

- You are feeling insecure around others. For example, you think you are too tall, too short, not intelligent enough, etc.
- Whenever you figure you've accomplished something incorrectly or you don't know something, you feel slightly awkward in social situations.
- You can't take constructive feedback and criticism, and you are constantly reacting.
- You fear others will hurt you if you get too close to them.

Pessimism. It is a general view that everything is wrong with you and with the world. When your outlook on the world we live in is negative, individuals who incline toward pessimism may likewise feel defenseless and accept that any moves made are probably not going to generate a positive result. Pessimism makes individuals believe themselves to be passive beings on the planet and, to a great extent, will attribute any chance of accomplishment to factors that can't be controlled.

- You think life is always full of pain and disappointment.
- When the phone rings, you assume the caller will be a bill collector.
- You fail to recognize the positive aspects of life.
- You fear making mistakes because of the catastrophic events that'd happen after your mistakes.
- Self-sacrifice is the belief that the needs of others should come at the expense of your own needs.

- You think that it is better to sacrifice your own needs or desires for someone else.
- You like to prevent others from feeling the pain to avoid the guilt of being selfish.

If you have any of these vulnerabilities, it might be difficult for you to see things with a rational mind and from a logical perspective when conflicting with a narcissist. In addition, by taking into account your vulnerabilities, you give the narcissist less power to control your emotions.

The narcissist's conduct is not the slightest bit your fault. Nobody has the right to be controlled, utilized, and abused. Despite this fact, the narcissist will regularly make you believe that you are at fault and deserve to be used.

It's vital to note that a relationship is a two-way street, like the biological example of a parasite and a host. The parasite can't work without its host. So you will need to do some self-reflection to make sense of what you're getting from your relationship with the narcissist.

Sometimes, your physical home or family may be at stake. In different cases, the narcissist's attention on you may be, to some degree, soothing regardless of how destructive this attention gets. Perhaps you like specific characteristics or have tender memories with the narcissist, or maybe despite everything, you believe they can genuinely change.

You have to access whatever emotional vulnerabilities you carry, assess them before pushing ahead so you can close down a narcissist for good. Therefore, when a narcissist comes and pushes a button on any of your vulnerabilities, give yourself space to catch your breath and interrupt you going into defense mode since you are now aware of your weaknesses.

You can gain control of your emotions with empowering thoughts or sayings like:

"I will take a moment to calm myself down so I can respond to this (event) rationally."

If you have a personal relationship with the narcissist, phrases like these will help you:

"I suggest that we postpone this conversation until you have had a chance to calm down."

"It is clear that you are used to taking charge and having things go your way, but it's not okay for you to dismiss my opinions and feelings."

When you adjust your mindset instead of being defensive, you can respond assertively. For example, in professional situations, you can say these phrases to help calm the situation:

"I'm ready to work this out with you, but I am not willing to be insulted by you."

"I would like to maintain a respectful working relationship with you, but I'm concerned with...."

"You are entitled to your opinion."

"We see things differently."

"Let's talk when you are feeling calmer and ready to stop yelling."

However, by a wide margin, the best answer to repelling a narcissist is that we should all acknowledge more frequently. Narcissists don't empathize with others and put little effort into making people around them hopeless and miserable. In half a month to a couple of months, they can make everyone around them ineffective. Furthermore, narcissism is difficult to change. Thus, if at all possible, simply keep yourself away from the narcissist.

Don't for one moment think you are more intelligent than the narcissist. Just keep your distance if you can.

Chapter 11:
Healing from Gaslighting

A narcissists will influence your friends, family, and coworkers to turn against you and isolate you. His charm and persuasiveness turn your circle of influence into his own little "hive" – people who now buzz around him and believe everything he says about you. This is the worst damage he can do, and while you can successfully escape the abuse, this damage can take months, years, or even decades to recover from.

The victim will feel rattled after having gone through something akin to what a prisoner of war suffers at the narcissist's hands and his hive. The hive, which has never experienced these things, will not understand or believe what the victim is talking about. Instead, they will think that the victim's experiences are "made up", "fake", "imagined.

The abuse victim is again thrust into abuse at the hands of others who do not seek to understand his or her experience. They are not afforded even simple understanding and validation for the experiences they have gone through.

The victim is confused about whether or not he is the victim or the perpetrator of the abuse, having been blame-shifted by the narcissist and the hive. So the narcissist and the multitude flips into victim mode themselves to mirror what the victim is projecting.

There is power in numbers, and the hive knows that yelling more loudly than the victim will make the hive and the narcissist seem like the victim instead. So everyone comes to the aid of the wounded narcissist and his multitude.

People naturally want to side with those who are popular, and it is easy to see that no one is taking the side of the narcissist's victim. This decides to side with the victim an unpopular decision, and no one wants to be on the unwanted side. The victim will be reeling once they realize that the narcissist has even stolen support from their inner circle, which is the final nail in their coffin.

Most victims of gaslighting and narcissistic overt and covert abuse retreat to lick their wounds. They are devastated to see that opinions and ideas are so fluid and so shifting in the wake of the narcissist.

Their perception is the truth of what happened; however, no one else subscribes to their version of reality. Even worse, other people will seek to convince actual victims that their reality is false, contrary to their own experience and their own eyes. This leaves victims of gaslighting alone primarily to heal their wounds. Instead, they must rebuild their own lives and their future.

Victims must reclaim their lost identity in the wake of the narcissistic abuse and the attack from the hive. Victims must reach back into their childhood to reassemble the broken pieces of who they once were and seek to define a new identity that can be reborn from the ashes of the devastation left by the narcissist and the hive. Victims must move forward to build a new arsenal of memories from newly created experiences, adventures, and memories in their lives. They must live with intention. They must live with purpose.

Abuse victims must find a new purpose after the devastation from the hive and the narcissist. They must discover and work on their own goals and positively support others.

Most survivors of narcissistic abuse go on to tell their stories. They go on to warn others of abuse. They go on to protect and advocate for the victims of domestic violence and narcissistic abuse. Finally, they educate others about the abuse they have experienced from the hive and the narcissist.

They go on to define the things that they have felt, thought, heard. Then, they warn others that the hive is coming for them and help them build a wall to protect themselves against the multitude.

The survivors must band together to fight narcissistic abuse and gaslighting. They must be there for each other to support and encourage one another.

Survivors must form their hive and a protective barrier together against the multitudes of the narcissist. These new hives must have ethics and morals and loving inclusion; however, they must not open the door to the narcissists and the multitudes that power their disorder.

The Future for a Narcissist and You

What does the future hold? Nobody has a crystal ball, but the bottom line is this - if you are in a manipulative relationship, the only realistic option you have is to get out of it and work towards righting the damage that has been done. The future will continue as the present is now, and chances are the

manipulation, and its damaging effects will become worse still. Manipulation and psychological abuse do not just stop; they continue onwards and snowball effects to the point of no return.

There is no future for a relationship of this kind. As sad as it is, and as much as you may not want to hear it, that is the truth.

Breaking up is hard to do, nut Always the Right Thing

A "regular" relationship, i.e., a relationship that isn't affected by narcissism and manipulation, is difficult to end. If you're the person doing the ending, you might agonize over your decision for months; you might question if you're doing the right thing and tie yourself up in knots. Then, when you finally end the relationship, you might regret it for a while, wonder if you did the right thing, and second guess your actions. This is normal.

So, when a selfish or manipulative relationship is forced to end, you're going to feel the same emotions, but with even more confusion thrown in for good measure. Breaking up is always challenging, whether you're the one doing the breaking up or you're the one being broken up with. If you could walk away from such a relationship with ease, you would be heartless and lack empathy yourself, possibly making you a borderline narcissist!

For that reason, understand the feeling of grief when the relationship ends with making a mistake. Breaking up is hard, but in this situation, it is always the right thing to do. There is no way you can continue in a relationship that causes you upset, psychological, and emotional damage and causes you to doubt yourself and your sanity constantly. That isn't healthy and isn't loving.

It's easy to say you deserve better, but everyone does. Nobody deserves to be manipulated and abused in this way. This is the cruelest way to treat a person: to cause them to become a shell of their former selves, to take a vibrant, full-of-life person and turn them into someone so lacking in confidence and self-assuredness, they don't know which way is up or down. That isn't someone who loves you. That's someone who wants to control you and manipulate you.

It's also challenging to get your head around that someone, a human being, would cause this much pain to another person. That is sometimes the reason why people stay in these types of relationships because they can't quite fathom why someone they thought so highly of could act in such a cruel way. The problem is that the person they thought they knew isn't the natural person underneath the mask.

A narcissist doesn't have the same feelings as a regular person, and they don't have empathy, which means they don't feel guilt or remorse when they hurt another person. For example, an average person would feel guilty or bad if they saw someone they cared about crying, but a narcissist doesn't have this in them or if they have a clue of it, it's not enough to stop them behaving the way they do.

A narcissist is never going to develop empathy without very intensive therapy, and that's something a true narcissist is not going to do. Without acknowledging a problem, treatment won't work, and narcissists do not believe there is anything wrong with them.

So, what options do you have? You can carry on in the relationship and hope things improve. However, the chances of that occurring are incredibly slim. So the other option is that you can leave the relationship and work towards a brighter future. For your own sake, we hope you choose the latter.

Why a Narcissist Will Never Be Happy

A narcissist, a true narcissist, has a personality disorder, and unless they seek treatment, they will never be free of the constraints which the condition imposes upon them.

When you look at narcissism from the outside, without actually knowing anyone with the condition or being a victim of someone who manipulated and abused, it might be easy to feel sorry for narcissists. They do not have empathy and therefore cannot love in the same way. They don't feel things the same as others and can't connect with others in the same way.

Due to the complex effects of this type of personality disorder, narcissists will never be truly happy. Their constant need to control other people and their continuous self-centered thinking make this type of lone wolves.

The future for a narcissist is much the same as it is now. Empty. Cognitive-behavioral therapy and deep mindset training are the only ways to overcome narcissism. Still, this first requires acknowledgment of the problem and a willingness to work hard to overcome it. Unfortunately, a narcissist is highly unlikely to admit they are wrong, so they're not going to realize they need help because of their entire personality traits either.

This means that most narcissists will continue in the same way for the rest of their lives. Friendships will fall by the wayside, relationships will start and end, and people will talk about how they were manipulated and hurt by them. It's sad to think that help is out there but rarely taken advantage of; but again, you can't force someone to face a problem if they refuse to admit it's there in front of them.

This truth, however, should not stop you from walking away. Yes, it's sad that a narcissist will never indeed be happy, but you need to focus on your happiness.

Your Future Will Become Brighter Over Time

What you need to hold onto is the fact that your future will become much brighter over time. It's almost like someone has a remote control in their hand, and at the moment, the brightness setting is shallow, almost to the point where you can't see what's on the screen. The brightness will remain low until after the break is made, and at some point immediately afterward, the

brightness might dim ever so slightly further, but only for a second. After that, it's as though someone is slowly turning up the brightness a notch every day until you finally reach a point where the intelligence is almost blinding.

You will get there, but you have to give it time. You have lost someone you love, and you need to grieve that fully. But you also need to unravel the manipulation you've been subjected to and straighten out your mind once more.

All of this takes time, but it's time well spent. Your future does not have to be the same as it is now. It can be brighter, and it will be brighter if you take the brave step to break free from the clutches of manipulation, putting the brightness control back in your own hands.

Tips:

- To be happy, you need to extract yourself from a psychologically and emotionally manipulative relationship.
- If you stay in the relationship, your situation will remain the same or may even worsen.
- A narcissist will never be happy because people will continually leave them due to the abuse they subject people to.

- Narcissists are unlikely to change because they will never admit there is a problem and get treatment.
- Your future will be brighter if you make the break, but you need to allow the grieving and healing process to happen, which all takes time.

You deserve better!

Chapter 12:
Learn to be Strong

D o they see you weak? Why you and not someone else? Maltreatment is selective, or so it seems to those who have been victims of some kind of bullying. The abuse can come from your partner, your friends, or even your family. The abuse can surprise us at any time and catch us completely unprepared.

Maltreatment can be as physical as it is verbal. We must never forget this detail because verbal abuse is probably the most widespread, as it is the most difficult to identify. It is so veiled that sometimes we cannot understand who our attackers are because their violence lies in their words. The objective of the action defines the difference between aggression and maltreatment. Aggression is determined by the lesion it causes, while mistreatment is described with submission, humiliation, domination, fear, slavery.

It is straightforward to say but more challenging to do, and this the aggressor knows well. For this reason, always try to take advantage of situations that leave you completely speechless. It surprises you! This way, you won't know how to react. Until a similar situation occurs again, you will not know which fish to take. You feel confused, sometimes even lost, and you have been so surprised by the actions of the aggressor that you are almost in a state of shock: it's completely normal. Sometimes the situation is more significant than you. Different and varied situations that you never expected to happen, much less at the hands of that person.

If you don't, nobody will. Believing in yourself is not a matter of pride but personal dignity. It is that psychological bond we cling to every day to trust our decisions, stop being afraid of misunderstandings, and allow us to get up a hundred times. To believe in ourselves is to love each other with courage, knowing that we deserve something better.

However, suppose these four words are seen so often in the windows of bookstores, in manuals and specialized magazines. Then, for a particular reason, the human being struggles enormously to trust his abilities, enhance his virtues, and believe in his possibilities.

As we have already said, the best thing to do is not to play his game. This is why your reaction is significant because that is how the aggressor will know whether to leave you alone or continue. How to fight an attacker:

1. The aggressor will bring fear into you. Use it to think fast, to stay awake, and to know how to respond. Do not allow the fear to paralyze you or bite you.

2. Be convinced and doubt all the orders given by the aggressor. Don't let him know that he has power over you. Who is he to give you orders?

3. Be sure of yourself. Self-confidence is something palpable and keeps any offender looking for a victim away.

4. Don't be aggressive because that's how you will enter his game. The important thing is not to be either too submissive or too aggressive. A balance between the two is the best thing.

5. Non-verbal language betrays. Stay calm, look into each other's eyes and keep your eyes fixed.

There are indeed people who are more exposed to abuse than others.

For example, some people oppose verbal abuse and, for this reason, become victims of physical aggression. It is something that is always talked about, but then, out of fear, few act. If you think you are unable to prevent abuse, seek help! Some people can help and support you. You are not alone.

Learn to say "no," learn to know what you want, what you don't want to allow, and what you deserve. Safety in yourself scares off the attackers. High self-esteem and unbreakable security will be your best weapons to make the attackers escape and prevent them from approaching you.

No one has the right to make you feel small

Knowing the meaning of the word "self-esteem" is essential to learn not to confuse it with the concept of mood. We often tend to attribute the reason for an individual's change to external factors such as the actions of others or circumstances, using phrases like "someone or something has diminished my self-esteem." In reality, self-esteem depends only on ourselves.

By definition, the word refers to the consideration that everyone has towards himself, that is, the ability of everyone to love each other. Thus, self-esteem is the perception one has of oneself. Being linked to the individual himself, the consequences related to the concept of self-esteem cannot fall on any external agent.

- **Self-concept.** It is the image that each individual has of himself, based on ideas or beliefs related to his person.
- **Self-respect.** It is how each person respects their needs and values and the way they face and resolve their feelings and emotions.

- **Self-acceptance.** It means accepting oneself for what one is, in one's own being different from all the others, appreciating one's own merits, and acting to improve one's defects.
- **Self-evaluation.** It consists of the ability to evaluate one's own behavior and form of acting, with sincerity and fairness towards oneself, to learn and continue to grow.
- **Self-Knowledge.** No one knows us better than ourselves, with our qualities, abilities, weaknesses, flaws, and limitations.

How is self-esteem generated?

There is no doubt that the concept we have of ourselves in our lives as adults come from processes originating during childhood. For example, our self-esteem stems from the image the people we grew up with projected onto us and the kind of relationships we have had since birth.

If our relatives have been interested in our needs in the past, giving us love and affection and showing us how important we were to them, the image that no doubt has been generated in us will be positive, exemplary, or we will have a "high self-esteem."

If, on the contrary, we have spent a childhood marked by emotional and emotional deficiencies in relationships with those around us, and if they have not been able to show us the good that is in each of us, we will probably have grown up with little consideration of ourselves, developing "low self-esteem."

One cannot be happy without being in tune with oneself since unhappiness arises from dissatisfaction with not knowing who one really is or considering oneself incapable of everything. Making self-esteem grow therefore becomes a necessity for emotional survival.

When our levels of self-esteem are low, we need to seek in others that degree of appreciation, consideration, and support that we are unable to give ourselves. In this way, getting that recognition from others will make us believe that "our self-esteem has grown"; in doing so when others disappoint us or do not behave as we expect, we tend to think that they are "lowering self-esteem mistakenly."

Yet this is not how it works. No one can change what lies within us. No one can lower or increase our self-esteem because if we feel the need to seek the approval of others, it means that self-esteem was already low by itself.

What is meant by mood?

The soul is an emotional state that changes according to the moment, circumstance, and other factors; for this reason, we can feel happy, sad, or unlucky with relative frequency. The mood is something of a passenger. When we do not get what we expected from others, for example, esteem or gratitude, our emotional state of mind is negative.

However, our state of mind is independent of our self-esteem since it is inherently low when we feel the need for others to remember us, what we do well and what they think of us.

Despite being a much more stable and profound component of our state of mind, self-esteem can be changed. It will require a more extended period to be changed, i.e., the time necessary to modify the image one has of oneself. It is possible to learn to increase low self-esteem through therapies that teach us to penetrate our inner life. It can also happen that you pass to try a negative perception of yourself due to a disturbance or a personal problem that affects your consideration from having high self-esteem.

If this is the situation, the cause is, above all, how we build our internal reality. From childhood, we shape ourselves based on the stimuli we receive and the interpretations we make of them. In this way, and based on what others tell us or project us, we build a stronger and more resistant sense of identity or, on the contrary, a more vulnerable ego.

Believing in yourself is not easy when your environment does not help in this regard. Likewise, relying on your skills is not easy when we focus more on our failures than on the sense of overcoming. And it's not easy to project a solid and courageous sense of identity if they taught us to focus on what others are doing, on what they say or think, rather than paying attention to ourselves.

Therefore, assuming responsibility and control over ourselves, we can decide to restore our self-esteem and get in tune with our person, learning to love and appreciate ourselves for what we are. By doing so, we will enjoy a whole and happy life, even though others do not like it as we are.

Chapter 13:
How a Gaslighter Will React When You Resist

H ow will someone who's been gaslighting you react when you start to resist? Above all, how will he or she behave if you break the news to them that you are leaving when you've been in an intimate relationship with a narcissist?

Well, I must be honest and say, "Very badly." The truth is that facing this challenge is one of the difficult things you have to do to defend your peace of mind. Not only have you had to suffer from their usual bad behavior, but when they start to lose control over you - especially if you announce that you're leaving - they will behave worse than before.

Before explaining why this happens and what you must prepare yourself for, I want to answer a question asked by many: Do you tell a gaslighter that he is "a gaslighter"? Do you say to a narcissist that she is "a narcissist"?

No! What are you thinking to accomplish by doing so? To make them see the error of their ways? All that has been explained to you in this workbook, and so many other writings by psychologists, make it clear that the "Cluster B Personalities," as they are referred to, don't feel any kind of responsibility or remorse. They refuse to see their faults. They are also hypersensitive to any criticism, and accusing someone by labeling them with these terms is hardly giving them a compliment, is it? Are you still thinking that you have to find a sufficiently good reason to explain why you are resisting their gaslighting tactics, to justify your leaving them, or at least, no longer co-operating? Forget it. You must make your own decision and follow through with it. Another thing to remember is that these types of people love playing the victim: your labeling them as a gaslighter is simply going to spur them into trying to convince everyone, you included if possible, that they are the victim...and you, the abuser! You don't want to give information to people with these kinds of personalities: they see information as a weapon to attack you with, not as the means to find the truth.

You need to recover and look after your inner thoughts and yourself. If you can leave and have decided to do so, don't think that you are morally obliged to announce it with a blast of steel trumpets. There is no goodwill in a narcissistic personality that obliges you to behave as you would, openly, with a normal person.

The reaction of your abuser to you resisting their efforts to confuse and weaken your beliefs, to make you reject your feelings, has to be understood as the manifestation of what sort of a person he or she is. He thinks he's the best, the cleverest, the most unrecognized man in the world. He feels envy and is deeply competitive. He's terribly sensitive to any criticism and so becomes violently protective of what he sees as being his rights. Anything that might go wrong in his business, intimate relationship, or family is YOUR fault.

He tries his utmost to believe he is always right, always. He will never look back over his day and ask himself if he did the right thing, because whenever he goes where he wants to, he thinks he's where he should be all the time. When he's not...it must be someone else's fault. He doesn't see a need to understand himself: he may feel there's something "other" lurking inside him, but he's in no mood to open a can of worms, and it's far easier to convince himself that he knows himself perfectly.

Cass Geistlichter is an actor in his own play; he is the hero and in the audience, all at once. He hates even the thought of being weak or vulnerable, and so he seeks power all the time. He's proud, haughty, and sneers very often. He enjoys harming and abusing you because it makes him look stronger and better than you. And he is a CHILD. Deep down, despite his memory and intelligence being those of an adult, he's a sulking, self-centered, spoiled child!

If this person, or his female equivalent, senses that you've changed, that you've seen through his actor's mask, that you're resisting, he will strike back. If a country goes to war, the army has to plan for it and to do so, they have to look at what material and personnel they have and at what they know about their enemy. I say to the victim of gaslighting: do the same! I'm not advising you to go to war in the sense of attacking your abuser in the same way he or she attacked you, because you can see by now that this doesn't work. The illustration here is that you must prepare for the conflict by understanding your abuser. You must know what you can expect.

Gaslighters are people who fear rejection. They do realize that their actions would cause other people to reject them, I believe. This is exactly one of their reasons for trying to make you passive and dependent on them so that you find it harder to resist. It's just as true to say, in contrast, that a gaslighter is dependent on you! Also, they are highly suspicious of others, knowing that many people (really, almost everyone) do not have the sky-high opinion of them that they think they deserve. Their personality traits make them defensive, and their arrogant lack of concern for others makes attacking their best form of defense. They don't have a clear idea of their behavior having any effects, and if you should announce that you're going to leave or that you have, it will be seen as an unprovoked attack.

So how will they react badly? They will react with fear and frenzy if they are very dependent on you. They always wanted you to take all their insults personally, just as they will take your resistance to them as a personal insult. They will usually attack.

I have to distinguish the types of possible reactions of a gaslighter rejected: the attack is a reaction of a person who is dependent on, who still wants his or her victim. Another possibility is that the victim is still "narcissistic supply"; in other words, the victim still gives power, validation, and service to the abuser, but the abuser will try to play a game of false acceptance. He or she is trying to surprise you, perhaps sensing that you were braced for an attack and hoping maybe their false surrender will unnerve you. They may also hope that that you're still bonded to them in trauma and are going to start missing them and grieving once the familiar patterns of your life suddenly end. You've actually had a lucky escape (for now, at least, your abuser may change tactics).

There may be another reason for an abuser to react with indifference: he or she might have been at the point of rejecting you! A male gaslighter who's been unfaithful to his wife for some time, for example, may have found her "replacement." If she's the one who asks for a divorce, he takes advantage to make it look as if he's the deserted one! A female gaslighter who reacts unexpectedly calmly is, I think, even more likely to have her male partner's "replacement" all lined up.

However, most gaslighters will feel totally betrayed and will be really angered, hurt, and panic. The more immature he or she is inside, the worse the feeling will be. I can't "sugar-coat" this bitter pill...

The abuser is likely to do some or many of the following: insult you, de-humanize you, say the worst and most personal things they can think of, use everything they know about your weaknesses to exploit you; they'll make out the best thing you ever did for them was an attempt to hate them, and they'll try to punish you as if you were a child, to destroy anything they know or think you like. They'll try to use other people to hurt you, will tell lies about you to them. They might threaten or stalk you. Physical violence happens in some cases - especially if your abuser has resorted to physical aggression before.

You need to plan what you will do. If you cannot leave the partner, colleague, or family member who gaslights you, then you need to make your resistance a covert operation. Using the "gray rock technique" is recommended, although once a narcissist senses your resistance, you will have to resist more openly. Just do it as calmly as possible.

One of the things you may see when you look logically at the behavior of a gaslighter who's been spurned is that he or she lives in a world of fantasy. Facts are warped, stories told, and lies rule. This must steel your resolve to heal yourself and will serve as a justification for your playing games with your abuser, which both leaving suddenly and the "gray rock" approach are. You have to protect yourself from abusive, delusional people; don't let anyone try to make you ashamed!

It's going to be a struggle, but as I said, it's mostly a battle on the inside, the battle to heal yourself that you started in the very first moment when you realized you'd been gaslighted and that your abuser was - an abuser! So in the face of the list of evil deeds and actions that are possible reactions of a narcissist who's been unmasked and resisted, you have to say to yourself, "I DON'T CARE WHAT THEY SAY! I DON'T CARE WHAT THEY TRY TO DO: I'M NOT TAKING THIS PERSONALLY! I'M NOT LISTENING TO ANY OF IT". Then go ahead and cut off any means of communication such as social media that your gaslighter might use to send you abusive or lying or threatening messages.

The attack could be open and in the public, or private and secret. It could be both at the same time. Whatever it manifests as, please do not take any of it personally. When other people are used as "flying monkeys," don't lose your temper with them. Give them a reasonable answer if it's called for, but avoid giving information if that's what they've been sent to do. Really, don't lose your temper in any of this. Too often, losing your temper is thought of as being a successful way to react to aggression, but it's a sign that you've "lost your cool" and that your abuser has power over you. You can be angry - you have a right to be if you've been treated badly - but being angry, and screaming and shouting and insulting back, are not necessarily the same. You can be angry but controlled; seek to be like that.

If you have children with the person who gaslighted you, and you leave, think carefully and caringly about how to handle them. Be calm, and explain what you have to explain to them without being apologetic.

Your abuser may very well play the victim: other people may be presented with tear-jerking, hysterical performances where you are accused of being crazy, unfaithful, and cruel. Narcissists will quite literally accuse their victims of doing whatever they have done to them. This includes calling YOU a narcissist! When other people are taken in – and, unfortunately, they often are - you have to be absolutely determined not to let their views change you. Handle them politely and insist that they do not know what you do. They don't have to see what you saw or suffer what you did. In some cases, other people are co-abusers, such as you may find at work or in a family.

Oh, I nearly forgot, your abuser might try to "love-bomb" you again. If all else fails... The common thread in all the possible reactions is not even apparent abuse, but games, games, and more games. So be clear about that and do not respond to the "love-bombing" because, as you know all too well, it's not real love in any way. You are likely to get the good old abusive reaction back again, i.e., "I invited you, and you just threw my invitation into the trash!!" Answer calmly that an invitation is just that - not a command - and it can be refused, which you prefer to do.

Yes, you've had to deal with a "child": a child's rages, sulking, and tantrums, combined with adult knowledge. Your "child" may even play by putting on a grown-up disdain and appear in public with his or her new "dolly-girl," "toy-boy," "Mommy-Substitute," "Sugar Daddy," or whoever; but it's all a disguise of a childish attitude. Treat it with contempt likewise - the contempt of an adult who really doesn't have to be vindictive and really doesn't need to waste time on childish silliness! If you face danger, be a brave adult and don't tell yourself that it's better to tolerate being gaslighted because you are facing a challenge. You get nothing from being confused, weakened, and destroyed slowly; nor does anyone else. Abuse has to stop. Sail into the future of recovery and have a fuller, more meaningful life!

Chapter 14:
Self-Care

N o matter the improvements you notice in your self-esteem by applying the suggestions, it is almost impossible to completely free yourself from the negative impacts of gaslighting as long as you continue to engage the gaslighter. One mistake common of gaslighting is trying to play the role of an expert therapist. You are not a therapist; you can't change anyone (even therapists don't change anyone), so don't even attempt to change anyone.

However, it is rarely the case to have gaslighters seeking help, especially in romantic relationships. Many gaslighters are mischievous narcissists with sick minds and can hardly recognize anything wrong with their behaviors.

If you must regain control of your life, trust your judgment, become psychologically and emotionally balanced again, then you must cut off any contact with gaslighters. First, you must completely dissociate from people who make you doubt your instincts and judgments. Then, you must consciously create an environment that supports that "inner knowing" where you feel something is off without anyone making you think that you are crazy, too sensitive, or overreacting.

Taking steps to rebuild your self-esteem and recognizing your true self-worth is essential. However, it is equally vital to engage in practices that can help you piece your life together again.

Your Inner Talk

There is a massive difference between leaving an abusive relationship and healing or recovery. Cutting all ties with a gaslighter is like removing a piece of clothing. You're not going to walk around naked, just like you're not likely to stop relating to every other person. You need to put on another piece of clothing; you have to associate with other people. But if you don't make inner changes, you can still inadvertently get into another abusive relationship or partnership. Stop expecting others to change for you to have a better relationship. The changes must begin from you—deep within you. For this reason, you must make concerted efforts to change your inner self-talk. Consider using the following exercises.

Thought-Awareness Exercise

Most times, our thoughts are on auto-pilot, and this is mostly a good thing. It will be unrealistic and unhelpful to monitor every thought you have because that is impossible and more than a full-time job! However, if most of your thoughts are negative or self-sabotaging, then having those thoughts on auto-pilot will do you more harm than good.

Living or associating with a gaslighter for long can make your thoughts predominantly negative, especially thoughts about yourself. To make matters worse, if you have endured a gaslighter for a long time, you have likely habituated these patterns of thoughts that almost feel normal. But you can change all that, beginning right now.

Deliberately take several pauses during your day to notice the contents of your thoughts. Then, mentally take note of what you are thinking about yourself or write down your reviews if you prefer.

Observe the thought without criticism or judgment. Notice the idea irrespective of how it makes you feel—good or bad.

Now, write down a short statement that describes the thought. For example, "I am thinking of how stupid everyone will think I am if I tell them how I feel."

The next step is to challenge or question that line of thinking by writing down several statements that will dislodge the negative thought. In the preceding example, you could write challenging ideas such as, "Really? Everyone will think I am stupid? How do I know that?" And "I've got some great friends and loved ones who understand and support me. They'll tell me if they think I am making a mistake, but they definitely won't think I am stupid." Continue to add as many affirmative statements as you need to reinforce positive thoughts and diminish any negative thoughts and perceptions about yourself.

Self-Interview Exercise

Have you ever been in a hot seat? Have you watched a show where someone was in a hot middle? Well, this exercise puts you in the hot seat with an interviewer. But in this case, you are both the interviewer and interviewee. So, you will be answering questions from no one but you. To help you remember the self-interview exercise, set timers to go off at different times a day. The duration for this exercise is entirely up to you, but I recommend doing this exercise at least twice daily for a minimum of five minutes.

Mirror Work

Mirror work (not to be confused with shadow work) is a powerful exercise designed to reconnect you with your core self and rebuild your self-esteem. For example, gaslighting may push you to begin to think that your world is falling apart. Mirror work can correct that impression to make you start to see a meaningful world around you again.

Victims of gaslighting have a difficult time being intimate not just with others but with themselves because the gaslighter has eroded their self-confidence. The mirror work puts you in touch with yourself again by making you stare at your reflection in the mirror.

To practice the mirror work, you will need to:

- Do the practice for at least five minutes each day in front of a mirror.
- Use a private space where you will not be disturbed throughout your exercise.
- Create meaningful, believable, and positive affirmations that apply to you directly. Vague or general affirmations can be a colossal waste of your time and effort, no matter how positive they sound. You can say things such as, "I believe in myself," "I trust my intuition," "I am wise," and "I trust my abilities." Make them short, powerful, and believable. Don't include words such as can't, don't, not, won't, and other terms that negate in your affirmations. For example, instead of saying, "I am not weak," or "I won't give up," say, "I am strong," or "I am steadfast."

The process is as follows:

Stand in front of a mirror (your dressing mirror or bathroom mirror will work just fine).

Maintain eye contact with yourself for at least five minutes. After that, it is okay to blink, but continue to look at yourself for the duration of the practice.

You may feel uneasy, embarrassed, awkward, or emotional during this process, which is okay. Just lock eyes with your reflection and allow yourself to take in all the emotions.

Repeat your personalized affirmations while staring directly into your eyes. This can help to reprogram your self-talk.

This exercise can reconnect you to your inner child and shift your perspective to one of innocent and empowerment.

Shift Your Self-Perception

You are not a loser, even if gaslighters want you to believe otherwise. The following suggestions can help you change the way you see yourself, from a weak, fearful, and powerless person to an empowered, strong, and self-confident person.

Do Something Off-Limits

Gaslighters will make you believe that you can't do a thing, you are not good at something or you are incapable of comprehending anything meaningful. But that is all part of their lies. Whether it is a hobby, career, or an experience you've always wished to explore, go right ahead and do it. Begin to break all limits (real or perceived) that Gaslighters have placed on you.

However, it would be best to keep in mind that you do the things you want to do because you genuinely enjoy doing them. Doing something because you want to spite a gaslighter only shows that they still have control over you. Act out of your conscious free will and not because you have a point to prove or want someone else to feel bad.

Help Others

This may seem a little bit far-fetched, especially for someone trying to get back on their feet after surviving an emotionally abusive relationship. But helping others, even in small ways, can help to boost the production of oxytocin, dopamine, serotonin, and all the other feel-good hormones in your brain (*Psychology Today*, 2014). Interestingly, the level of your feel-good hormones is linked to your willingness to help others. In other words, the more feel-good hormones are released in your brain, the more you will want to help other people, and the more you help other people, the more feel-good hormones are released. It is a chain reaction.

Emulate Habits from Role Models and Mentors

Find people with qualities that you appreciate and emulate them. Instead of listening to a gaslighter, find role models and mentors who will repeat empowering ideas to you repeatedly to reinforce your belief in yourself.

Chapter 15:
Self-Love and Self-Care

S elf-love and self-care are not about being selfless. They're about accepting that you exist. It all started on an average day...

You may have even felt your first inkling of self-love through being around someone who loved you unconditionally. You can quickly think that this person, or something universal, created the love you felt for yourself. Maybe it was feeling like the only other person in the room for once. Or perhaps it was having all your needs met through that person; maybe they would listen to you and meet all your needs without demanding anything from you in return at all times.

When you were selfless, they acknowledged that you exist, and you felt love. But why did they buy your existence? Maybe it was because you were kind enough to meet their needs without demanding anything in return at the time. Perhaps you did something for them to make them feel good about themselves. Or maybe it was just because they were able to see the goodness inside of you and wanted to help bring out the best in yourself by loving and accepting you, as is.

You deserve love...and so does everyone else. You probably know that when someone loves and accepts "you" unconditionally that it feels good. It feels good to move forward without needing anything in return, especially if someone is doing it for you. No expectations are put on them either, no strings attached. They just love and accept "you" because they care about you (maybe more than themselves).

If you were in a relationship with this person, you may even have felt like they would be the person to protect you from the horrible world because they've put their trust and love in you. You may have felt that their love was all you'd need for security and stability. If someone is putting themselves first more than they are putting you second, they don't deserve your love or respect.

Chapter 16:
Overcoming Gaslighting in Relationships

G aslighting is a common tactic in emotionally and physically abusive relationships, and it's a betrayal of essential trust (Gattuso, 2019).

Dealing with Gaslighting Parents

Suppose one suspects that one's mother or father (or both) is gaslighting one. The tips are:

1. Confide in a trusted individual about the manipulation: A child can go to a trusted adult, perhaps at the place of worship or school, and describe some of the things that bring concern. As an adult, you'll need to think about being able to go to a trusted friend or family member that you can openly talk to about what you're experiencing.

2. Maintain healthy boundaries: A child may need to establish firmer boundaries with parents to prevent them from impacting one negatively. It is also always advisable to have less contact (or no contact) with parents where possible and necessary if it would help. The same applies to adults. You need to make sure you're setting boundaries or considering what your boundaries are and what is and isn't acceptable in a relationship with you. You can think of boundaries as being the minimum level at which you want to be treated.

3. Talk with a psychologist or professional counselor about one's concerns: Counseling can help repair the family if possible.

The child can enter psychotherapy or counseling, or the whole family can be seen to help change this unhealthy dynamic. Perhaps, if the parents know that it is hurting their child, they will hopefully stop their acts; however, this is unlikely because most parents do not view such actions as problematic behavior.

4. Visiting a family therapist to potentially correct this unhealthy dynamic: although complicated and involving lots of courage, it is important to discuss or uncover your parent's manipulative behavior with a professional.

Dealing with Gaslighting Friends

While facing gaslighting as a child comes with its own range of pros and cons, the same applies when dealing with gaslighting among your friend and social groups. Some of the best ways to combat friends' manipulation include:

1. Understanding the severity of gaslighting: First and foremost, one must realize this emotional manipulation tactic's seriousness as gaslighting is used to help the manipulators or gaslighters get their way every time. The fact is that gaslighting is severe and not a game; hence, you should not allow a friend to gaslight one. Look for consistency and regularity in your friend's actions.

2. Set firm boundaries: No matter how minor the gaslighting from a friend may seem, it is paramount to set healthy boundaries as soon as possible (such as not borrowing from them, not entrusting your children or pets to them, etc.) and inform such friends about the negative impacts of their behavior to you and the boundaries you would enjoin them to

respect if the friendship must progress. If they oppose your decision, then it is a clear indicator that they value neither you nor your mental health, and that's hardly a friendly behavior. This is where you'll start to figure out whether this is something you actually want in your life.

3. Give them time to adjust: You may find out that your friend is going through some stuff at home or is trying to grow as an individual, which means you could actually support their recovery journey rather than just cutting them out of your life. If friends show respect and a genuine effort to uphold your decisions and respect your point of view, it is safe to say they value your presence in their lives and genuinely want to put effort into your relationship. Hence, it's a good idea to give them some time to adjust to your new boundaries. Just keep an eye on what is happening to make sure they are actually putting effort in. Remember, actions speak louder than words.

4. Behavior: Whatever caused your friend(s) to start gaslighting could be out of their control and beyond your understanding, but that still doesn't make it acceptable. Therefore, you must keep an eye on those subtle behaviors that don't seem to change to prevent a doorway for more significant manipulation. Note that gaslighting has a snowball effect, and the longer you stay in it, the more severe it tends to become.

5. Make a tough decision: The most challenging part of a relationship is knowing when to end it. This is a mature and weighty decision to make but must be made at some point. You can't simply put up with it forever. When they don't follow or respect one's boundaries, you might need to step away from the relationship. This could involve staying away (that is,

cutting all ties with them) or acting bored or ambivalent such that they walk out first.

6. Consult a professional: Finally, if you are unsure about a particular friendship or need some additional guidance when dealing with them or moving on, you should consider talking with a mental health professional or a therapist, as friends can sometimes be skewed in their opinions.

Dealing with Gaslighting at Work

Gaslighting in the workplace can be difficult since you spend so much of your life there, and it's a very public space where you'll have managers and colleagues from all walks of life around you. However, several steps can be taken in dealing with a gaslighting boss, employer, etc., which include:

I.   Get grounded in your truth: Gaslighting is all about distorting your sense of reality. This means it's necessary to sit with what you know to get yourself back, grounded in reality, once experiencing gaslighting. Trusting yourself is the key to coping with this toxic behavior and identifying what's real and what isn't. Pay attention to what the gaslighting is telling you so you know what you potentially doubt yourself about.

II.   Keep documentation: Once you feel gaslighted or harassed at work, it is necessary to keep documentation of what happened in memos, emails, dates, times, people involved, direct quotes, and other evidence proving what is happening. Do not keep this data on a work-issued device, as the company may have access to that data and will take the device upon quitting the job or may have access to the files to manipulate. You can't simply believe that a manipulator won't do this. One should not trust one's memory as verbal proof and is nowhere near as impactful as digital or paper forms of evidence.

III. Ask colleagues if gaslighting is also happening to them: Sometimes, a gaslighter(s) at work will focus their abuse on one employee, but they often see many people in their path to power and will gaslight them as well along the way. Therefore, it is good to find out about the gaslighter's interactions with colleagues. If they also receive similar treatment, one could ask them if they are willing to document the gaslighting behavior. This helps one from being the only one making a complaint since strength lies in numbers.

IV. Do not meet with a gaslighter alone: You must be very cautious of private meetings with gaslighters; instead, you must consider bringing in a trusted co-worker or another supervisor as a witness. If the gaslighters refuse to allow another person in the room, ask for the reason and tell them of your uncomfortable feelings. Additionally, if you have to meet with a gaslighter alone, you must ensure proper documentation.

V. Know your rights: You should learn your workplace protocol (if any) for reporting harassment. An attorney, especially one specializing in workplace rights, can give you legal advice and recommend what steps you should take to guard yourself and if you have a potential harassment case against your employer.

VI.   Consider leaving the job: Yes, it is unfair to quit your job due to someone else's deplorable behavior.

Dealing with Gaslighting in a Romantic Relationship

Ending any romantic relationship is never easy, and perhaps the hardest breakup of all is with a gaslighter because as you're leaving, they pull you in, and once you're back in, they push once again, keeping you in a state of limbo. However, these are some steps you can take to deal with gaslighting in a romantic relationship that can help things get better, or can help you leave entirely and start working on building a new chapter in your life:

A. Break up in one quick conversation: If you're choosing to break up with your partner and simply want to get out and move on, the key to a successful separation is making it fast and precise. Tell the gaslighter that the relationship is not working, and as such, it is over in a straightforward, calm, and direct voice. Also, try to avoid language that offers an opportunity to make alternative decisions that the gaslighter may use to change your mind. Believe me, they will try.

B. Don't believe promises to change: Immediately, as you put a halt to the relationship, your former partner may try to win you back by tendering instant apologies and promises that things will change with words that sound authentic and genuine. They'll try and remind you of how beautiful the relationship was at the beginning and what you're potentially missing out on. A part of you might want to believe them. However, it is all part of the manipulation, and you should not give in to their words or pleas. The unhealthy relationship dynamics will return and, perhaps, get worse. If you've tried to make things better several times and it turns out the abuser isn't changing, or even putting effort into growing, then it's time to call it quits and get out.

C. End all communication: Once the relationship has been ended officially, cease all means of communication (such as blocking their phone numbers, emails, accounts on social media, not picking up calls from unknown numbers, etc.). They may also try to enlist mutual friends in their effort to reunite; you must tell them to desist from discussing the gaslighter, and if they refuse, you may need to simply walk away from the conversation.

D. Ask friends to remind you of how bad things were: Even when you know breaking up was for the best, you might still grieve the end of a relationship that seemed so promising. With things like social media, it's sometimes hard to avoid people. You may see a picture and start doubting whether you made the right choice, and perhaps you want to go and see if they're going to try the relationship again. This is when depending on your loved ones, social circles, and support groups come in.

When thoughts of giving the victimizer a second chance creep into your head, your support network will remind you of the horrible past and that you deserve better. In the absence of friends and family, group therapy (helps you realize that you are not alone in situations like this) could be beneficial. You can even flick back through this book or through the notes you've made to remind you of everything you wrote down and how you felt. One excellent technique one lady using was that she walked away and wrote a letter to herself at the end of her relationship. She wrote about how awful she felt in the abusive relationship and how empowered she felt finally walking away. Whenever she had the idea to reconnect, she reread the letter.

E. Make a list and check it in moments of doubt: Hand in hand with the letter-writing idea above, a simple checklist can help dramatically after a breakup. Write down all the times you felt gaslighted during the relationship and read through it whenever doubts about just how poisonous the relationship was or when hopes of reconciling arises. The list will remind you that the relationship was unhealthy and unworkable and reaffirm your commitment to stay away from them forever.

Dealing with Gaslighting in Marriage

It may not be pleasant to deal with a gaslighting spouse—you may even tend to ignore such a partner—but if you notice it early, the following tips can make dealing with it much easier and will help you have the power to make your own decisions and protect your well-being:

a. Respond to their malicious claims immediately: Arguing with a gaslighter is vain because they'll gaslight at any given opportunity and conveniently make it look like whatever it is you're talking about is your fault. More so, a gaslighting partner is never going to understand your side of the argument.

b. Second-guessing is not an option: Dealing with a gaslighting spouse can be overwhelming, but you must have confidence in yourself. At any given claim of a gaslighting spouse, it is essential to pause and think if what they are accusing you of is actually true. There is a massive difference between your belief and what you are being pressured to believe; therefore, understanding the distinction is vital in surviving gaslighting. Make sure you're keeping proof of things happening if you suspect gaslighting is taking place so you can check and have a sound state of mind.

c. Keep yourself grounded at all times: A gaslighting spouse will tear down your sense of thought and foundation to lose your idea of individuality and engage in their games of manipulation. Therefore, you need to keep yourself grounded and not let your spouse's hints, doubts, and gossip shake your belief in yourself and everything around you. Having control of your emotions and thoughts can help you deal with a gaslighting spouse better. Mindfulness meditation and journaling are a fantastic practice since you're literally training yourself to be grounded in the calmer times, which allows you to remain grounded during the stressful times where you may be experiencing heightened emotions.

d. Closely focus on the accusations: Seeing if there is any credibility in what a gaslighting spouse is throwing at you will aid dealing with such accordingly. For example, if you are being accused of cheating on your partner or bold claims are being made that you're lying to them, all you have to do is take a step back and analyze if you have done anything to incite those accusations. If not, then the chances are that your partner is the one who is engaging in the act, and this will give you a better grip on the situation and help you deal with the gaslighting spouse.

e. Confront them with the problem: A gaslighting spouse may pretend they are listening. Eventually, they'll blame it on you or that have been misunderstanding things, and that all their accusations and other gaslighting personality behavior were simply out of care and concern.

f. Seek professional help if things get worse: A counselor or therapist will help you see your relationship's downfall in a better, more productive manner and even guide you with some strategies to deal with your gaslighting spouse. They will also help you rebuild your confidence, walk you through grounding yourself better after the relationship has ended, and even help you reconnect with your true, genuine self.

g. The last resort to deal with a gaslighting spouse is to leave them: if you have tried everything and can't make any progress, then it's time to leave and let go. However, sometimes things in a relationship just can't get better. There's too much negativity in the past, too much resentment towards each other, and too many built up, habitual emotions that you'll both need time and space to let go of. Quitting a marriage can be a bit of a process, but if it's the right thing to do, know that you're taking a bold step into a new and happy life that you can build for yourself.

Defending Yourself against Gaslighting

Of course, regardless of where you're experiencing the gaslighting abuse in your life, several tips are important to remember if you're looking to defend yourself, protect your emotional and mental well-being.

a. Recognize the abuse is present: This is often the first step to protect yourself from gaslighting. After all, you can't fix what you don't know is broken. Once you are aware of being manipulated, you can determine your reality more quickly.

b. Don't take the blame for the other person's actions: The other person may claim you provoked the abuse and that it's all your fault ("You made me act this way"), but it's important not to give in to their claims. You are never making someone else act a certain way. Even if you make someone so angry on purpose, they still always have a choice in how they operate, just like you do. If you should avoid the actions that offended them in the past, the gaslighter will likely develop new excuses for their abuse.

c. Don't sacrifice yourself to spare their feelings: The other person's desire for control will never be fulfilled, even if one dedicates their whole life to ensuring their happiness. People who gaslight others are usually trying to fill a void in themselves, but they will not fix their hearts by breaking yours.

d. Remember your truth: The mere fact that the other person sounds sure of themselves doesn't mean they are correct. It's just a good performance. The gaslighter may not ever see your side of the story yet; their thoughts do not define reality, nor do they explain who one is. Their view on life, just like everyone else's, is subjective to them and is usually a reflection of how they see themselves.

e. Do not argue on their terms: You are unlikely to have a productive discussion if the other person is fabricating facts. You may expend all your energy, claiming what is real instead of making your point. The abuser may use gaslighting techniques to declare that they have won an argument, but you do not have to make conclusions based on a defective premise.

f. Prioritize your safety: Gaslighting usually makes targets doubt their intuition, but if you have a feeling of danger, you can always leave the situation. You do not need to prove that a gaslighter's violence threats are sincere before reporting them to the appropriate place. It is often safest to treat every risk as credible.

g. Remember, you are not alone: You may find it helpful to talk about others' experiences. Also, therapy is a safe place where you can talk through your feelings and memories without judgment. A therapist can help to recognize healthy and unhealthy behaviors, teach you how to resist psychological manipulation, and in some cases, help to develop a safety plan for leaving the relationship.

Conclusion

To be trapped in the narcissistic snare of trickiness and deception is comparable to being a fly caught in the cobwebs. When entering the web, does the victim realize that it will be bound up and eaten alive by anything other than the fly? The appropriate response is "no."

Deciding to move on and leave the web does not mean you don't cherish your partner, boss, or parent. It implies you esteem reality and are more passionate about opening the door for you to be more joyful, more confident, and surer of yourself as an individual, regardless of whether it implies separating. The ill thing about gaslighting is that it takes place more regularly than you might expect.

What's more, it works so well that you would be astounded to discover that scholarly and straight-thinking individuals fall victim. Your relationship with this individual that once appeared as though paradise has now ended up being terrible, and it's something that nobody wants to admit, making it even harder to accept.

There is no harmony or euphoria living your life in this position, when all that is left inside you is a constant dread and unending desire for concealment. Your life has lost all expectations, and, as though the light has been killed, all you see around is murkiness and the profound dark haze of melancholy. You are currently compelled to live in a condition of passive consent to endure.

The gaslighter's deception constantly subverts your perspectives on the truth, so you wind up losing trust in your instinct, memory, or thinking powers. These are spun lies that disclose to them that they are over-delicate, envisioning, absurd, nonsensical, over-responding, and reserve no option to be vexed. Their existence is turned back to front upon hearing this on numerous occasions, and they start to accept this may all be valid.

The narcissist's with his/her psychological abuse and oppressive practices has figured out how to ingrain in their victim the extraordinary feelings of uneasiness and disarray to where they no longer trust their memory, recognition, or judgment. In this state, they are a prisoner. Nonetheless, many figure out, usually with a bit of help and guidance, how to discover and obtain the fortitude to break free.

Yet, these are generally after a few problematic endeavors. Yet, when they do at long last break, they may discover their way to the therapy room in time. Remaining in a toxic relationship can break our spirits. However, acknowledging that you deserve a better relationship where you are treated as worthy and receive the level of respect that you and all human beings deserve? That's liberating.

You fully deserve and have the right to be in a stable relationship where you are regarded and treated with affection. You ought to never need to bargain for somebody who doesn't treat you right. There is another person out there more suited to providing for your needs and will aim every day to treat you better.

More critically, delayed toxic connections can have enduring, negative consequences for our psychological wellness, constraining us to feel useless or irrelevant. Given time, you'll be able to release these negative feelings and reverse the effects, but you need to find the courage to take that first step.

I'm hoping you've found this book useful, and it's giving you absolutely everything you need to identify, highlight, overcome, recover from and deal with the gaslighting in your life, and basically how to tackle any kind of toxic relationship you may find yourself in, both now and in your future.

CPSIA information can be obtained
at www.ICGtesting.com
Printed in the USA
BVHW091504140621
609529BV00007B/1961